MW01297503

Life As Art

The Club 57 Story

STANLEY Z. STRYCHACKI

iUniverse, Inc.
Bloomington

Copyright © 2009, 2012 by Stanley Z. Strychacki

All rights reserved. No part of this book may be used or reproduced by any means, graphic, electronic, or mechanical, including photocopying, recording, taping or by any information storage retrieval system without the written permission of the publisher except in the case of brief quotations embodied in critical articles and reviews.

iUniverse books may be ordered through booksellers or by contacting:

iUniverse
1663 Liberty Drive
Bloomington, IN 47403
www.iuniverse.com
1-800-Authors (1-800-288-4677)

Because of the dynamic nature of the Internet, any Web addresses or links contained in this book may have changed since publication and may no longer be valid. The views expressed in this work are solely those of the author and do not necessarily reflect the views of the publisher, and the publisher hereby disclaims any responsibility for them.

ISBN: 978-1-4401-4752-4 (sc)
ISBN: 978-1-4401-4753-1 (e)

Printed in the United States of America

iUniverse rev. date: 5/25/2012

Life As Art:

The Club 57 Story

Life As Art: The Club 57 Story is a memoir of and beyond the years 1977 through 1983, the lifespan of Club 57, a small venue that had a major impact on the Punk/New Wave popular culture movement, and through it, all of Western society. A disproportionate number of significant artists emerged from this church basement at 57 St. Mark's Place in New York City's East Village, including painters Keith Haring, Kenny Scharf and Jean-Michel Basquiat, photographer Tseng Kwong-Chi, actress and performance artist Ann Magnuson, and performace artist John Sex.

Life As Art: The Club 57 Story is a 64,000-word memoir. Its primary readership will be all those interested in the development of popular and avant-garde culture in the extremely fertile period that stretched from the late 1970s into the mid-1980s. Since the effects of that period are being felt quite strongly now, we can expect that the age groups of most such readers will span the 20s, 30s and 40s.

Of particular interest to today's readers will be the chapters dealing with the abovementioned trio of painters, especially Keith Haring, whose legend appears to grow daily. Indicative of this phenomenon is the upcoming Broadway musical show about Haring, which will open in 1998, called "Radiant Baby." More than this, a large number of young people involved in pop culture today, both as producers and consumers, are fascinated with this period of New York history. For these, *Life As Art* will be essential reading.

Life As Art: The Club 57 Story was written by the club's creator and director, Stanley Strychacki, who emigrated from Poland in 1972, looking for freedom and adventure, particularly the artistic variety, in America. Working with the young people who were instrumental to the flowering of the East Village, he became fascinated with their energy and idealism, and devoted himself to furthering their creative work. Stanley Strychacki is the first to tell the story of Club 57, from his unique point of view as the surrogate father of a cultural Vesuvius.

Introduction

People like to know the circumstances of culture. Where Picasso and his colleagues gathered for lunch, for example. How African ceremonial dance steps survived the centuries to appear in today's pop music videos. Or how the Agora of Athens served as a meeting place for Plato and his students. Did the shape of the market's stones, the liquour of the café, the dust of the stamped earth, flavor the produce of these minds? Curious about the people who have molded our own perceptions, we want to know how they lived, how they were. And we hope that, knowing what we can of these circumstances, we will be able somehow to fit their extraordinary doings closer to our own framework of logic, to ease our awe, our fear, perhaps, of their power to change us.

Did Club 57 change us? It's not in the general lexicon as a mass culture landmark, the way bigger venues like the Fillmores East and West and Studio 54 are. Only a few thousand people might, if chancing to walk by the church on St. Mark's Place, think of something unbelievable they once saw or did inside. A few thousand more might get the same reaction walking past Irving Plaza, remembering when the club took over the old Polish wedding hall to host rock bands and the New Wave Vaudeville show.

But Club 57 ultimately affected millions more than ever stepped inside one of its events. Created in a low-ceilinged basement, the social hall of a tenement-sized church in New York's East Village, the club, along with other forces in New York and around the country loosely grouped under the heading of punk and new wave, cold-cocked a decade floundering in fatuousness, making way for an era that paints its icons warts and all, and gets a good laugh out of the picture.

The experiences of Club 57's director Stanley Strychacki, as recorded here, briefly describe many of the artworks and performances that were shown and created therein. But this is not the overriding purpose of the book. Works by the more renowned artists, such as Keith Haring, Kenny Scharf and Jean-Michael Basquiat, are more fully explicated in art history books and museum and gallery catalogues. But here, these and less celebrated works are interwoven with the circumstances of the club—how it came to be, how the participants interacted, and how the things that happened were able to happen.

The last of these holds the biggest key. How was it that what appeared to be a punk rock club, filled with visually outrageous, verbally incitive and overtly sexually experimental young people, was allowed to operate for five years in the basement of a church? And how did the members come up with night after night of performances, art shows, film festivals, group activities and extensively casted productions—a new program nearly every night, and all this without any of the Government-sponsored funding that is so bitterly and publicly fought over today.

The short answer is that author Stanley Strychacki was able to appreciate the members' attacks on nearly every aspect of society as part of youth's mission to reinvent the world. More than that, the author could hear in their outbursts the cries of those too untimely ripped from their childhoods by an alienating mass society, who fought back with merciless satire and parody, keeping at bay this monster they would soon need to embrace. It was a cry as well against the solutions of their older siblings, whose '60s-based optimism had by the '70s been degraded by mass culture into a Pollyanna of indiscriminate protestations of love and acceptance. Slaying this syrupy dragon was the first order of business to drag the national mindset into the present.

Stanley saw that it was worth the effort. Seizing the moment, he melded the energies of these young people into a support structure that kept them afloat as they did things too innovative, too bizarre for patrons and foundations to support.

As we join their outings and extravaganzas, their explorations of sexuality and reckonings with life and death, we begin to see that it was the glue of human lives that held together the club, that made it possible for so many to palpify their fantasies and nightmares. Sometimes this glue gave way: for many it was with their lives, spent in the excesses of the time, that they paid.

This is the part of living on the edge that's not so much fun: falling off. But in another sense, straddling the edge was what Club 57 was all about: as Ann Magnuson once described herself, "one foot in sarcasm, the other in sincerity."

-Leonard Abrams

Contents

Chapter One

The Bells Of Saint Stan

They ring every day at 6pm at the St. Stanislaus Church on 7th Street between Avenue A and First Avenue. That time for me is the most secret and sacred time of the day. The sunset, the calm, and the strange feeling of unknown yearning and nostalgia comes to my heart, my soul and my mind. That special time of day when even my body wants to participate in thirst of unknown immortal happiness with somebody whom I want to touch and hold, full of love for the world, humanity, nature and the spirit of goodness. The twilight comes slowly, moving on the city streets, then on the roofs of buildings until at last it touches the Empire State Building. It covers the daily life of its pedestrians, and the inhabitants behind the Venetian blinds and curtains. I often close my eyes and I dream about that secret love that is mostly not accomplished. Then my heart sings a song of melancholy for an unknown dizzy dream. Then I think how many people have the same feelings at that moment.

But even though the night covers the view of people's faces, the voice of bells comes everywhere behind secret curtains to the most secret secluded places in the city and in our hearts. The bells ringing like the beat of my heart together with them, falling on the East Village. Wherever I go—to stores, to restaurants, to clubs or to the subway. From the beginning of this chapter I wanted to look at the East Village from a high building, from where one could see the streets around here. But there are none here. And the towers of the churches are small, hardly higher than the roofs of the houses. Only the sound of those bells can go everywhere, where neither the towers' shadows nor the rays of the sun can go.

This sound can tell you where it was and what it saw and took with it across the whole city. And what it whispered back to the church tower from whence it came, and to the bells from which it was born.

I have lived many years in the heart of the East Village on St. Mark's Place. St. Mark's Place is actually 8th Street, but between Avenue A and 3rd Avenue, it has taken that name from the St. Mark's Church which stands on Second Avenue and 10th Street. Whew, it's probably too much for you, but that's how it is.

This street was the most Polish Street in Manhattan just a few years ago. If you walk from Broadway eastward, then you will see many crowded places between Third and Second Avenues. That was where the Polish National Home was, now the Rehabilitation Center. There is still Twardowski Travel Agency and across the street is the Polish barber.

One block further, between Second and First Aves, there is the Polish Catholic Church under number 57, which gave its name to some Art Club in 1978. And under number 56 is the Polish Democratic Club, while close to First Avenue was the Theater 80 St. Mark's. On its roof you still can see the Polish national symbol, the White Eagle. Then on the next block is the Polish school, with its St. Stanislaus Church, which goes through to 7th Street—there were several Polish stores and offices.

But now only the White Eagle remains, the last sign of Polish society on St. Mark's Place. The same thing happened to Little Italy downtown. Looks like those natives made enough money and moved to better places to live, and they left behind them, still alive in the East Village, a church and a few restaurants, including Teresa's, which has the best Polish food. I am still here. The people who live here have changed. And I really like them. There were Italians and Jews as well, but now the only ethnic community that remains is Ukrainian.

And how does St. Mark's Place look now?

Looking toward Broadway we see Astor Place, where the 6 train brings the crowd from Wall Street and Uptown. Lafayette Street and Fourth Avenue. converge here too, making the place very wide open. In the middle the Cubic Rotating Sculpture balances on one corner, and all the young tourists feel compelled to turn it on its axis. Off to the side, close to 3rd Avenue and St. Mark's place, sits the famous old Cooper Union Library.

I like this building very much because of its architecture and elevation, on which you can look without tiring your eyes. Its delicate decorative elements against the brown sandstone evoke the treasure of books within. It seems to want to tell to students and people passing: "Come to me, I am for you, I want to live in your mind! I will give you the best only somebody who loves you can give. I will give you my wisdom, nobility and dignity for whom the people will have respect and admiration, and I ask for nothing in return." That library imposes its character on the neighborhood. It puts its mark on NYU, the dormitories, on the traffic of the streets.

That library is putting its mark on the faces of boys and girls, which like a river flowing to St. Mark's place and past the library, smile to her with yearning for the wisdom and knowledge hiding within her walls. And probably no place exists in the world like here, where in this river of people you can spend a long time and not see anyone older than 30. It seems not long ago that I was one of them, could move my head looking for the happy faces of my friends and the expression made by thier clothing and manners. The boys and girls cross St. Mark's Place, and it is more a parade than just walking to their apartments, clubs, restaurants.

St. Mark's Place is like their living room. It is the most prosperous place. Here you can choose books and records, you can buy the best punk clothing, accessories and jewelry. In this block is my favorite restaurant, that small Japanese restaurant called Zen, where I like to meet my friends. Here you can buy old books and magazines from a table on the sidewalk, along with Indian incense, if the smoke from the cars is not enough. Life here flourishes 25 hours a day, and you can feel safer here than at home. Here at the curb you can see the most decorated motorcycle in the world. It should be in the Museum of Modern Art together with its owner, who looks like his vehicle.

Motorcycle gangs like this street too. I had two motorcycles myself once, and I loved them as much as a cowboy loves his horse, or maybe like a boy loves his girl. I don't have it anymore, but you know that really love is eternal, isn't it? Don't tell me you don't believe in love.

Start to love your vehicle. I miss that time very much because I was so young, I was 20 when I got that bike, and will always remember the country roads and trackless earth and whistle of wind in my ears, caressing my cheeks.

Let's go to the next block of St. Mark's Place, between First and Second Avenues. It is the quietest of these blocks, maybe because there are not too many stores. Instead there are three churches, two cafes, Orlin and Jules', and the Pearl Theater Company. They give this block social character. There are many beautiful acacias growing here, climbing plants on the houses, which fill this block with nature, grace and charm. Here at #57, in the basement of the Polish Catholic Church, from 1978 to 1983 was the smallest and perhaps the most creative club of the 20th century, if I may say so, the East Village Students' Club, on which steps the members would sit and drink Bud and talk about their financial, sexual, artistic and life's problems.

The great artists Keith Haring, Kenny Scharf and Jean-Michel Basquiat came together here, with their many friends, including me, Stanley, the first witness and admirer of their youth and creativity.

There is also that shoestore, whose wall contains a mural by Arnie Charnick. This artist painted many commercial advertisements at many stores around here, and his work really speaks to me. Near the corner often you can see a beautiful girl. Her eyes are like eyes from a Modigliani painting. Everybody knows her, including the police from the 9th Precinct. Once she walked these streets like ballerina, causing even the cops' mouths to water. She doesn't exist anymore, or maybe that's her, but she is so out of it that she doesn't know if she is hungry or not. It doesn't matter to her. But she is looking at another corner, where Stromboli Pizza is, where Ann Magnuson with her friends from Club 57 liked to eat a 50-cent slice of pizza.

From where the girl stands you can see the St. Mark's Bar at the Southeast corner. It has its own history, and not always a good reputation, but now it's a pretty cool place to have a drink after you visit the East Village. On the other corner is the Old Dutch Cleaners. Not very interesting, but right outside of the place is a heavy-faced, streetwise girl known as the Untouchable Girl or the Queen Of Smoke. She has run her business for many years right next to the kindergarten, teaching the babies how to be happy with dry grass for $10 a pack.

Anyway she has a few friends around her with little babies. They don't know that along with their parents they're selling grass, but at least somehow they share the profit—together with their uniformed friends who smile to them when they pass. We'd better go ahead, because the line has become long and she is busy. Now maybe we can hop to the Jaffa Café or to Café Mogador, both good, and on the same side of the street. At Mogador maybe we'll meet my friend Terry. He likes to buy grass from the Queen of Smoke, go to dinner at the Mogador, and go to see monster movies at the St. Mark's Theater. He used to have hundreds of friends, but now he is lost, good for nobody and nothing, just like the others, with the sick and lonely life of a drug kid; goodbye my child, I am going to see the Mojo Guitar Shop.

It's always nice coming here. They have the music Terry loved, and I can talk to the owner about anything. It's the friendliest music shop in the East Village. As soon as you pass the door of the store you already belong to the family of music. If you'd like to buy a guitar, or if you'd just like to have good conversation and don't want to buy anything, come here too—you will learn much about style, songs, places and events. The location, the clientele, the old-fashioned interior, and most importantly the owner, make you feel like you are with really good friends. And you can invite them for a cup of coffee, of course.

There are still more bars and coffee houses on this block. I don't go to every of them too often. From my bedroom window I can see café Sine-é, and Anseo, a bar specializing in poetry evenings. Often when I stay in my room or go to bed I fall asleep with a stanza of poetry in my mind. I like to listen to those voices; it reminds me of my childhood when I liked poetry very much. The tones of piano and poems relaxed my soul and inspired me. It's still not so bad in this world if youth still likes poetry.

It is still the poorest of the art forms, but rich in the music, life and wisdom of the people. If it is boring to you then look to your boring and poor mind. Poetry is the mother of action, art and inspiration for the best brains in human history. Tonight the bells of St. Stan pull me to the Anseo club; tonight the poet Anna Frajlich was reciting her poems. Her expressions, her lyric phrases were going to my imagination, especially this one:

"Beautiful is my mother,
Every spring more beautiful … "

It reminds me of my own mother, not because of the subject, but it touched my heart because of the expression, which made me see beauty from mother's wrinkles, and she has more wrinkles than years. It reminds me of her whole life, the work and pleasure that we shared, and the pain that we shared. She conquered America with me, and with her I trod down New York sidewalks looking for work, for the joy of New York life, from Greeenwich Village to Central Park. That gave us the idea in 1977 of creating and accumulating the street art at the tiny club in the East Village, when the East Village started to bloom together with the punk movement. Her smile was and really is poetry, and she gave that to the boys and girls when she was there talking to them. They were smiling and wondering, what is that older lady doing with us New York kids, and why aren't we embarrassed to be with her, but instead feel so good at her presence? She loved them, and they paid her in kind. She was so lovely, like Anna Frajlich the poet said at the Anseo bar.

That was my feeling, but how about the feeling of that girl who started to weep in the corner of the bar? What she was thinking? Where is her mother, and another thousand mothers of kids who are escaping every year from the houses of their moms? And why?

The next morning on the steps in front of the Anseo bar I saw a girl holding a handsome boy. It didn't look like they had family in New York. All they had was each other. She held him with her left arm and touched his hair and cheeks with so much love, in my mind more mother's love than lover's love, and it was so romantic and scenic, and the boy looked like he had been saved by an angel. I don't know if they'd already had breakfast, but I know it was the most beautiful picture I had seen in a long time. I even wanted to go down to the street to them and give them some money. It was well worth it to me, to satisfy my feeling of love for them. I didn't do it, I was too embarrassed to disturb them. I feel as if they were my own kids that I had abandoned, and I wanted to go to them and give them a hug and ask them for their friendship and offer at least the comfort of my life; but I didn't go to them. I tried to control myself even after I realized there was no need to. I thought I was being oversensitive, infantile, too emotional. Why do I have to be ashamed to be myself whole my life?

I have learned how to be hard and unemotional; I have played that role but believe it or not, when I was young I was the softest guy in the world.

That is why, when I first saw "Romeo And Juliet" on the stairs of Anseo, I knew they belonged to my world. I can feel it more and more, and I can do it only in the East Village, where I see here all kinds of people: many races and nations, smart and those not so, small and tall, punk and yuppie, mostly happy and wise and poor and so young and beautiful with their youth and grace, that remind me of my unfulfilled life and dreams. Now my best joy is watching them, happy with their ecstasy of life. I pushed my life so hard, and I had a life rich with excitement, not with money, because of adventures greater than Tom Sawyer's and Huckleberry Finn's, and all of them who walk on St. Mark's Place understand that. They are looking for a lost world of honesty, they want to give their lives to that research with proud head and spirit. They want to participate in creating a better world. And this is how my life was, which is why I love them more than anybody in this world.

You see? I told you—the voice of St. Stan's bells are taking my secrets and whispering them not only to its tower but also to the human beings like you. Why? Because you are the tower with your heart like St. Stan's bells, beating and ringing the song of your soul.

I've closed the window a little. I want to read this book and concentrate on it. It is about Michelangelo, and it's called "The Agony and the Ecstasy." I read it again, having had the time. He has become my idol even though he is not alive. But I am not sure if he isn't alive, he still is touching every human being of every age and nationality. He is not only my idol. I have to tell you that when I went to his grave in Florence I started to talk to him. I didn't ask him any questions, I just told him, "Thank you for what you have done for humanity, and for me personally, and I have a message for you. I registered you as a Club 57 member, aren't you happy?" And when I looked up to the head of his sculpture I could see he was more proud than just a few minutes before I came to the Church of Santa Croce. And I thank him for the

Pietà and his unfinished slaves, and the hands of God and Adam on the Sistine Chapel's ceiling.

The music and singing from Café Sin-é is coming to my ears more gently than balsam to a sore spot on my body. My eyes become tired and together with the poems and that music, I fall asleep with the book in my hands, hoping to have a nice dream.

With those two club/cafés generating this new style of social life, as do many cafés, restaurants and clubs around here, as well as several new art galleries, I feel like Club 57 has taken over the streets and I am in the middle of the club, but this time not working hard, just enjoying the East Village's inspiration and its new creations.

Just to the left there is another café/restaurant, Stingy Lulu's, and then Nino's Pizza. This is the one where I eat most often now. Its pizza beats any other's around St. Mark's, and besides it is so close to my apartment. I feel good around the people who eat here—this is my main kitchen, when my wife is too busy and can't make her delicious Chinese-American food.

The most architecturally attractive buildings in the East Village are the churches. It happens also that my building and the one across the street have those pseudo-classical cornices and windows unique to 19th century tenements. They're not really ugly, but rather make the building more esthetic than the lumpen popular culture of the time. Good, at least I can see one tree near the Anseo bar. The street is too narrow for me to see the sky. Then what makes this place romantic? Maybe the smells that are coming from the fresh bread of the Italian bakery on First Avenue, or Veniero's pastry shop and café, or delicious plates from the Second Avenue Jewish deli. Or maybe that garlic smell from the kielbasy in the Polish-Ukrainian butcher shop. Yes, the smell here is a special blend, especially from 6th Street, when so many Indian restaurants are packed every evening with diners from all over the New York area, seeking out the Indian spices and herbs that Columbus was looking for when he discovered America. Angelika's Kitchen, the vegetarian restaurant, also likes to use herbs too, but in the summertime, probably the best place to sit and enjoy a cup of tea is the garden at the Cloister Café on 9th Street near Second Avenue.

I can't tell you how many elegant restaurants we have here on Avenue A, the border of Alphabet City. The open space afforded by

Tompkins Square Park attracts many artists to this place. Noisy with children from kindergartens and boys playing baseball, the place is very alive and happy.

But it wasn't like that when two boys were killed a few years ago on my block by strangers who got bad ideas about the congenial people and atmosphere we have here, and there wasn't any love and common sense when the police rioted on my block and through Tompkins Square Park in 1991, beating our poorest people—the homeless, and those who had recently been released from mental institutions. I want this park for me and my neighbors' children too, but I don't want it by disregarding the rights of those who are society's casualties. There wasn't any democracy in this action, in this, the richest country in the world. That action of lawlessness was among the worst sins of our society. Do the police have as much energy to harass and chase the drug dealers? You have to answer that yourself.

The point at which St. Mark's Place meets Avenue A and Tompkins Square Park has a rich history in dramatic actions. Here under my window Mayor Koch did his famous commercials, "New York, Let's Clean Up New York." I liked that Mayor, and not only his pleasant face and character. There are some people about whom we say we can come to them without standing upon ceremony to give them a hug, because you can read in their faces friendship and directness—that's how I felt about him.

Here, at about 2 o'clock in the morning, suddenly you wake to a strong voice from the Greek coffee shop: "Shish Kebab, Shish Kebab!" He wants to make extra money to pay the high rent of his shop from clients who keep coming back hungry from meetings, dates, bars and nightclubs.

Here for a time walked a vagabond with a brown paper turban on his head. Everybody liked him, because he was so friendly and never bothered anybody. His brother had enough money and always wanted to get him to stay in his house in New Jersey and take care of him, but could he give up his village where his heart adhered deeply by the roots, and every tree and stone was his possession? Oh, he had very gentle and good eyes, that loved these dirty streets. He loved the people and the shadows of the people that passed and greeted him, and at moments you could see that his eyes brightened and smiled when he heard the well-known bells of St. Stan. That's why he didn't go to his brother, because love is stronger than anything in the world, and maybe because freedom to live one's own life is more important for a human being, like for a bird it is more important to be flying free than to have a gold cage full of grain.

Sometimes I think that I am attached and fastened to this village like that old poor man. I don't see him anymore, and it feels like something is missing. But people keep coming and leaving. If I were to build another statue in Tompkins Square Park I think I would build one for him. He loved this city not less than Mayor Tompkins, whose name was given to the park.

In this area I could see another older man, who had hair, moustache and beard white as snow. Kids at Christmastime were sure this was a real live Santa, because he didn't have a beard on a string. For this reason he was pretty busy and popular at the children's shows during that season. But I don't see him anymore either.

There was that couple, Adam and Eve Purple. Everything they had, clothing, hair, bags and their twin bicycles, was purple. People say she left him one day. But I still see him sometimes.

And then there was the man with eleven dogs, who would always walk them in Tompkins Square Park, and on St. Mark's Place. And the lady with the five cats whom she used to take out in a baby carriage.

I also used sometimes to see the one-eyed punk, John Spacely, who used to call St. Mark's Place his home. He often visited Club 57, and in 1983, filmmaker Lech Kowalski had his picture painted on the wall of a building on the famous strip between Second and Third Avenues for his film "Gringo." Spacely had too much fun perhaps, and died of AIDS.

But the Beautiful Girl and the Queen of Grass and her gang are still there, but I am glad they don't associate with this crowd of youth, mostly students, that walks down St. Mark's Place, the gateway to Tompkins Square Park, and then vanishes into Alphabet City. When I look at that crowd it seems to me they are angels sent from Heaven to walk here full of joy, untapped energy and vigor. I am happy after all that they passed that fat girl and didn't buy her product. They ignore her. They won't complain in the future about God and fate and who it was who ruined their life. They know that a brain was given to them to have responsibility for their lives, future and happiness. They know they have to use it as free creatures, because they are part of nature and God, and they were born to participate, to create a world better for them, their friends and family, society and the world. You can see it in their faces, from their books under their arms, from their musical instruments and their conversations. They fill up the cafés, bars, clubs and stairways in the front of the buildings around here.

In the East Village, sitting on the stairs has become both fashionable and domestic. Many are reminded of their home towns and evening traditions, where they spent many nights with their friends and family. I feel very good among them. I can talk to anybody here; this world is not spoiled yet. Here in the shadow of New York University, polished by hard life and thirst for knowledge, they are still hopeful and open, as they search for their place in the world.

Almost everybody here is without family or childhood friends. Everything is a new beginning. Poor and rich, lost and lucky—all have left their barriers behind them. They wanted new friends, new adventures, and they wanted to be together and belong to the great East Village Family. And it made them richer, and they gave most of their energy to make a new life in this part of New York, which became the sister of Greenwich Village and a base for NYU. But woe to those who find the wrong friends. Therefore if you're not into studying, join the Guardian Angels—they are the hope of America, too.

I have spent many days in the park with my mother and wife. But before I had my quadruple bypass operation, I played badminton there more than anything else. The park was very different.

The East Village was born in the 1960s during the hippie days, then went into a decline in the early '70s. But not for long. It started flourishing and pulsating with life again around 1977, when youths moved in again looking for cheap apartments. Then clubs opened their doors like mushrooms after a spring rain.

The Church of St. Brigid's, which stands behind the Park on Avenue B, opened its halls to all kinds of community activity. Rock music bands started to give free concerts in the Park's bandshell again, like they used to do in the '60s. Hare Krishna believers did their festivals and chanted their songs to the accompaniment of drums and tambourines.

And through the decades, May Day parades of American socialists and communists continued.

Then suddenly the Park became a huge camp for homeless people: vagabonds, bums, the mentally ill, the drug-addicted and the down-and-out. Soon the residents couldn't walk here and take their children to play. Everywhere it smelled of marijuana, urine and decomposing food, and worse.

The tent and cardboard houses made up a town of misery and despair in the center of the city where Wall Street governs the world's banks. From that vantage point, ill-considered decisions created psychic, social and moral conflict, the legacy of which we can still can see on the sides of walls: "Death To Yuppies," or "Police Scum."

I had come home just after 1:00 am. I couldn't understand why at that time there were so many people on the street yelling and screaming at the police. A helicopter circled over the roofs of my house and the buildings next door. The police had organized a powerful army on foot, in cars and on horseback. It wasn't easy to get to my apartment. It cost much explanation to the police to prove I lived here and I was going home. I just got to my apartment when my wife called to me, "Stanley, come to the window!" The cavalcade of police moved against the people from all sides.

The police moved against everybody they could find, most of whom were just standing around; against people who lived here and paid their salaries, supposedly believing they were protecting them. There were only few actual demonstrators there, because most of them had already moved to the next block several minutes before. The police were beating whoever they could find. I saw their victims shrinking and covering themselves with their hands, running from the police to the doorways of St. Mark's Place. It reminded me of the Communist militia in Gdansk in 1970, when thousands of shipyard workers and others demonstrated peacefully. They did it again, and even killed people in 1980. When I was able to go to Poland in 1989 I saw that place, commemorated with three big crosses and a placard with a quote from the Nobel Prize-winning poet Czeslaw Milosz: "You who hurt the poor man/The poet will remember ..." This beating of innocent people always comes back to my mind.

That night nobody slept in the East Village. That night will go down in the history of the city under "mature but not yet grown-up humanity." How did Governor Samuel Cox look at this from the podium of his statue at the corner of the park? How did the Greek goddess see it from her statue in the center of the park?

I wish that one day all the buildings on St. Mark's and all around the Park would be lighted like Christmastime at Disney World, and there would be lights in every window of the houses, and New Yorkers would stand here together in that light around the monument in the Park to understand that they can count only on themselves to be happy.

I wish there would be a festival of the art of friendship here. Martin Luther King had a dream, John Lennon had his "Imagine," and I have a Wish. Some new idea. At least I have not been killed yet. And it's good to have it at least in my "imagination dream."

I hope St. Stan's bells will never ring again as sadly as they did after that horrible night, but that their sound will reach the hard hearts not only in the back streets of New York but also to the farthest places of human nature, and will bind them to those words written on each of the four sides of the monument in the Park: Faith, Hope, Temperance and Charity.

So far the most attractive annual event at the park has been Wigstock, the drag queens' festival. I have nothing against that. They are nice people—that's why thousands of their admirers come here. And I even have a few drag friends. We have a good time. Now my creative life is different. I have a different life, less energy but still a high level of excitement, being an active observer but not a hanger-on.

And there are only lighted candles at two places near my building, where the friends of the boys killed here place candles in their memories, standing around looking at the red spot on the sidewalk and thinking, thinking.

I am coming from the swimming pool. I left the bus at Avenue A. There three youngsters, a girl and two boys about 17 look at me and say, "Yuppie!" Not angrily, but with a smile. Then I say to them, "If there were no yuppies, who would give you change?" I took $5 from my pocket and, handing it to the girl, said "This is for pizza." Their faces told me they were very thankful.

They ran together down the block, but passed Nino's Pizza. I tried to see where they were going, and why they didn't stop there. "We're going to another Pizza joint, better and cheaper," they explained.

They waved their hands and continued to run. How I wish they had run to school or work or home to see their families, but this is America.

This is vacation time. The young boy sitting next to Nino's made me laugh and amused me so well. He put a jar of water in front of him, and dangled a string on a stick into it. He looked at me with a roguish smile through the hair falling into his eyes. "Nothing's happened yet."

"This is your first fish," I said, and put a quarter into the jar. He was happier with his new invention and trick than with the money. Still the boy who wants to play with me. So I did. That is his living pop art, which is everywhere here: on the homemade posters informing you about their gigs and shows, on their clothing with fantasized forms, colors and details, even on all the street lamps decorated by "Mosaic Man" Powers, who takes broken porcelain and bottles, decorative stones, tiles and everyday things found on the street or in basements, and glues them to the lamps' bases. It is also seen in the spray-painted murals of Chico, the prolific street painter who has made all the East Village his mural.

The wind breathes from the west and brings the spirit of Shakespeare from the Public Theater, just behind the Cooper Union Library and La Mama Theater on 4th Street. It also brings the tones of jazz from street bands playing near the bank, the music of the soul that always is so close to me when I have yearning for dreams of the unknown, and thirst for unnamed destinations of my being, which is written on the front of the Cooper Library to Science and Art.

In 1972 I came to New York from deepest Poland—straight to 13th Street near Second Avenue, to the apartment of my uncle Walerian and auntie Betty Karwanski. I saw from the bus window the lights of this great city, like the Charlie Chaplin movie "City Lights," and they were throwing lights into my eyes like a cascade, like Fata Morgana in the African desert.

But the next day when I woke up and walked the streets of the East Village, suddenly I realized that I was in the ugliest city in the world. Where I am? Where is that New York? Yes, it was New York. Educated in one of the most beautiful cities in Europe, Gdansk, I realized I couldn't live here. These homes, buildings without any architecture or architecture from nowhere, struck my eyes as if somebody beat them with birches. In a few months I moved, escaped, to a little better environment, Sutton Place. And I never planned to come back. This wasn't my dream America.

And now I am here again, back from dead uptown to the fully alive new heart of New York, the East Village. So you see, it's true what they say: it's not important where you are—but who you are with.

Chapter Two

In The Beginning ...

"God created the Heavens and the Earth.
God saw that it was good."

Brrrrrrrring, Brrrrrrrrring. The phone is ringing.

"Good evening, Stanley speaking."

"Good evening, Stan. This is Father John. I would like to see you
at the Parish Hall. You know, we had a meeting about how to use the
downstairs social hall. If you're interested, I'd like to choose you to do
it. I hope I can convince you to do this."

And so it came about that Sunday in September of 1977 that Bishop
Jakubik and the board decided to give me that basement to try my new
invention, the East Village Students' Club, under the protection of the
church.

I saw the opportunity to create this center for students (and the
recently graduated and recently dropped-out), who were, first slowly,
then ever more quickly, moving to the East Village. I would use their
talent and enthusiasm to produce a series of social and artistic events.
Thus I would satisfy both the church's need for revenue and my own
hunger to produce events, of which I had done many in my life.

This has always been a real need for me, giving me a sense of
personal achievement, and adventure too. Little did I know how much
adventure was in store ...

I had come to the USA in 1972 with a head full of imagination to an unknown world. I was fascinated, not only with the capitalist nature of the society, but with every aspect of life here, so different from Europe—especially in New York. In this melting pot of people and cultures, everyone seemed friendlier and more relaxed. It's quite different than in Europe, which has been touched by two world wars and then, for many, the Communist totalitarians as well.

Soon after my arrival I organized a program for the Polish Cultural Center, which I called Renaissance. It was a success. We gave several Christmas shows with the great choir from New Jersey called Aria, to benefit blind children in Poland.

Eventually I left the Center, and worked for the Polish Olympic Committee in the basement of the Polish Catholic Church on St. Mark's Place. Now the Bishop of the church, John Jakubik, asked me to organize Polish parties and cultural events to raise revenue for the church.

I opened the club only three days a week at first, with people I had become friends with while living on 57th Street. These included singers Arlene Gold and Paul Wagner and a Canadian pianist named Doug McLennan. Saturday evenings I produced dances for the Polish-American community. As the days and weeks wore on, and more and more young people came to the new venue, I canceled the Polish dances and ran the club all week long. It gave me no satisfaction to do the Polish dances. I had to deal with the famous Polish tradition of drinking to excess, which I had no interest in.

In February of 1978 I was approached by some American youths who needed their own cultural club. Hungry to befriend these idealistic youngsters, for which I felt a great affinity, I changed the program, and Club 57 was born.

And thus began the life of this special place where we cultivated a unique atmosphere of artistic freedom based on love, acceptance and friendship, right here in the midst of bad, punk-fevered New York.

Many years have passed since. I myself have gone through several big changes. I got married, had a heart operation, opened a new business, and worked as a corporate employee. Similar things happened to others of the club generation. They went on to different modes of living, carrying with them the nostalgia for youth and its ecstasies. I decided to write about what happened, so that perhaps you will better understand that vibrant time, and the role Club 57 played in the East Village and the culture in general.

We had set up shop in the right time and place. There was the Bishop Jakubik with his liberal viewpoint, the empty church social hall in the basement, and me, a guy looking for adventure and friends, but the greatest part of the credit for creating the New Wave world of Club 57 I give to American youth. It was of course a special time in the history of American society. The Vietnam War was over, the Government had been rocked by the Watergate scandal, hypocrites like Jimmy Bakker and Jimmy Swaggart made money off the naïve with their bogus right-wing religion, the struggle against apartheid in South Africa was reaching its height, strikes raged in Eastern Europe, the Middle East was in upheaval—and all of this touched the minds of a new generation. And there was more afoot in the nation: Elvis Presley had died. Drugs had spread through America's cities and suburbs. The gay movement fought to reform the nation's primitive sex laws. And there were things that started right here in the East Village: the punk movement, the Guardian Angels, the East Village Eye magazine, and the concentration of youth and students with brains bursting with ideas, and poor youngsters who have nothing but energy and the need to release it.

These youngsters were so wonderful that I forgot all about the main reason I was brought in: to raise money for the church. I started to do my work at the club primarily for the sake of fun, friendship and happiness. I forgot about the fact that I had left the years of my youth behind in Europe. That period, for youngsters in New York, and those who came pouring in from the hinterland as well, was a time of great creativity, and what was coming from our hearts and our heads was more important than any calculated effect.

We weren't sure where we were going. Full of the excitement of life, and very headstrong, we were trying to discover the New Wave of everything, looking forward to an unknown future. I wanted the Club 57 kids' friendship more than anything else. My adoration of them and their work gave me great satisfaction. In this they never disappointed me.

The financial situation was never good. But Bishop John was quite understanding. Even though we fought all the way, he still allowed the club to remain for over five years. I don't know why. Maybe he got hooked on the young people's creative energy as well, or maybe he thought that one day it would become profitable.

Midtown had Studio 54. That was the place the rich and the wannabe-rich dropped many dollars in search of a good time. Here it was quite another matter. No money, but serious fun. Or maybe serious joy. For me it recalled the Bim-Bom experimental theater in Poland, which put on a satirical program named just that: "Serious Joy." It touched my heart as a teenager, and this feeling came back to me again. My club would continue in the same vein. Every year we would do more and more. And we did. Soon the bands couldn't all fit in the little basement. And that's when we started the Club 57 at Irving Plaza productions.

Then problems started to come to us. The wars with the church board, the owners of Irving Plaza, the neighbors, the police, the Criminal Court, "Noise!" "Perverts!" "Junkies!" "Free Thinkers!" "Free Lovers!" And so on.

"The art of the street." Yes it was. With complete love for everyone who hated us. The pressures grew. I couldn't sleep anymore, and this weakened my psychic condition. I fell into depression. It's not so easy to run an underground club. Taxes, liquor licenses, ASCAP fees—we couldn't afford these things. I was director of the most illegal club in New York, and I faced the challenge with stupid bravery and greatness. I had to work another job, as the club couldn't give me a salary. The IRS investigated me. They found nothing incriminating, but they were sure I was getting rich. Meanwhile we could barely find the money to buy toilet paper. Yet somehow the club flourished in spite of everything. Some nights we had three events.

Youths from all over came clamoring to express themselves any way they could, all with an overabundance of energy, talent and time. There were so many individuals and groups wanting to perform, that I could have opened ten clubs for them and it wouldn't have been enough.

Club 57 was in the center of the East Village. We got attention from all sides. We did live music, painting exhibitions, poetry evenings, storytelling, plays, fashion shows, break dancing, horror movies, rock'n'roll movies, cartoon screenings, parody nights, dance parties and wedding parties ... I don't remember what I didn't do. Each evening was another chapter. Maybe if I can find more time I'll tell you a hundred more stories. I was too busy running the club to get involved in the performances myself. But I would always dance—the moment I heard the music coming from the speakers. Jazz, rock, it didn't matter. I loved it all.

I'll never forget the crazy evening when the Fleshtones and the Zantees played the little club. Actually I preferred it to their later gigs at Irving Plaza and in the London clubs, when they toured while I was vacationing there. That evening was one of the best of my club life. That was the beginning for the bands, and for me too in this incarnation. We weren't spoiled yet by the events to come. I swear by the toe on my left foot that I never saw happier kids in my life, on or off the stage of Club 57. We will all remember well the way Peter Zaremba pulled from his harmonica the sounds of passion and paradise.

I did as many shows as I could with emerging groups. I had many discussions with New Wave groups, and also "Old Wave" groups looking to change their image, helping to shape them into the bands of the future. I didn't demand too much from them—just honesty.

Then along came Gordon Edelstein and Suzan Cooper. What a charming, friendly, intelligent couple. You wanted to do anything for those two experimental directors. Well, we put on "Cowboy Mouth" by Sam Shepard, who was just becoming established at the time. They brought new colors to the play and stirred up a lot of interest, packing the club for many nights in the process.

This was a rock'n'roll play, the fruit of a joint collaboration with Patti Smith. Written in 1971, it was an early attempt at combining rock'n'roll with theater, forging the way for megaproductions like "Tommy" and "Jesus Christ, Superstar." The story is actually a conversation between two lovers who argued about music, life and love, and how to find solutions and new roads in rock'n'roll.

The two characters, Slim and Cavale, have a strange relationship, in which Cavale wants to make Slim a star, because "People want a street angel, they want a saint with a cowboy mouth."

In this production, the Foolish Virgins, starring singer, songwriter and guitarist Steve McAvoy, closed the production with a set that showed plenty of love for rock'n'roll, as if to say the future was in good hands.

Soon after followed a production of "The Other Leading Brand" by Max Bloom, which ran for four months, featuring wholesome American humor. Then came "Kennedy's Children," written and directed by Robert Patrick. For the production, Robert changed the club into Phoebe's Bar, a place on 4th Street that still exists today, because that was where the action took place. The entire club became the stage. The cast sat among the audience, which became an integral part of the action. The bartenders poured drinks and said their lines at the same time.

A whole chapter could be written just about this play, which represented the generation that came of age after JFK's assassination, their hopes for a better world and the hard realities they had to face. And I agreed with the play's premise as I understood it, which was that the world would be a wonderful place if we allowed peace and love to flourish.

But peace and love are not immune to common errors. Once during this run when I opened the club during the day a little late for a scheduled rehearsal, Robert grabbed a chair and wanted to break my bones. I was shocked. I canceled the remainder of his shows. But we remained good friends. What can you do? Peace is harder to maintain than some writers would like to think.

I booked the rock bands only for the weekends. This way the music wouldn't interfere with the hardworking neighbors' weekday schedules. In spite of this, the police remained our most frequent visitors. People complained more and more. We didn't have money for soundproofing. Besides, it's not much of a solution for apartment buildings; it doesn't stop the vibration. This encouraged us to move to Irving Plaza.

I chose Chris Gremski as Club 57's first manager. Fresh from Poland, where he was an energetic worker in the solidarity movement, Chris was ready to do his best. Unfortunately, his totalitarian background did not always prepare him for the East Village way of doing things. But he took the job seriously, and with great pride and energy he set to work.

Chris got the shock of his life when we rented the club to a few girls for the huge sum of $200. We later found out why. They used it to hold a news conference, unveiling New York's first prostitutes' union. He was terrified of the ramification for the club, and I think probably terrified of being around all that sex for hire. He came up to me and said, "Stanley, I have nothing to do with this. Close the club immediately!" And he disappeared.

I was surprised too, but I took a cooler approach.

I went up to Bishop John's apartment and asked his advice. But it was too late. The reporters had already moved inside and started to interview the sexy girls. So the Bishop just waved his hand and answered, "We can't do anything about it. They're already here. But they are people too. And the church is for sinners. Let us listen to what they have to say."

So I went downstairs to the club. As I walked in the cameras followed me. The official inauguration of the union was wrapping up. The women had not offered any explanation of why they had chosen a church to meet the press. But the reporters did the best they could to inflate the issue. I answered their queries with a quote from the Bible: "Let he who is without sin cast the first stone." Then the girls explained themselves. Their time-honored profession, deserving of recognition for servicing the needs of many poor horny men, deserved certain minimum standards in the areas of payment, rest periods, health and safety. Our country compares unfavorably in this area when stacked against the sex industry standards of some of our sister nations.

The girls were friendly, neat and well-spoken. They came with their husbands and children. My mood soon changed from agitation to levity. I started joking with them, and as the press conference changed into a party, we started drinking and dancing together. Their behavior throughout the night was irreproachable. In fact, we became such good friends that the leaders of the group gave me their phone numbers. So, to quote Dr. W. Dyer in his book, "Your Erroneous Zones," "If you are shocked or horrified, then it's your problem."

Now to find Chris Gremski. Eventually he showed up, looking nervous and confused. I kidded him, "You see, Chris, you missed your big chance to be on TV." "So," he replied, "have you already become the union's president?" "No," I said with a sneaky smile, "But I got some interesting telephone numbers." Then the tension broke and we burst out laughing.

I will always respect that kid for his work against the totalitarian system, as well as the loyalty he showed me during the few years he worked for me.

Later I helped him to finance an anticommunist demonstration, of which Club 57 produced a radio simulcast, in front of the Polish Consulate. His serious personality did not help him to understand the free-wheeling nature of both clubs. Unionist or not, the prostitutes were too much for him to accept.

Every month the presentations at Club 57 changed, becoming more sophisticated. but the weekend rock concerts always resulted in police citations for excess noise. I had to go to the Criminal Court for a hearing. The Bishop armed me with letters explaining that the events were really "benefit parties for the church." Sitting in the cavernous courtroom were a few hundred people, mostly young. Most of them were there for selling drugs. I never saw such a fast tempo in a courtroom. It was a parody of itself. The clerk would call your name. You had to stand before the judge, who read the charge. You have to plead guilty, even if you're innocent. If you don't, you're really in trouble. Almost everyone was required to pay a monetary fine, after which the case was closed.

When my turn came I stated my case, then showed the judge my letters. He glanced at them, smiled and said, "Give my best regards to the Bishop." It looks like those high-ranking officials stick together. I performed this routine a number of times, killing lot of time in the process. Did I have any remorse? Oh, yes. I always felt sorry for that poor man on the other side of the club's wall. How much he had to withstand for the sake of art! He was so patient and understanding, and it seems that he liked the kids too. With much sadness in his eyes, he agreed on many occasions not to complain. He must have spent many sleepless nights in those days. It was I, with the aid of the rest of Club 57, who terrorized and abused this innocent man, robbing him of his rightful rest. He never even hated us for it. I am sorry, Mr. Blashko. I hope you can still be my friend. but I am sure that when you hear my name you purse your lips.

Eventually I stopped putting rock bands at the small club completely. But can you have a club without music? We kept the DJ. Well, at least a DJ is easier to control.

We had no problem with the Rock films series, the work of enthusiast Gary Balaban and his Cine Noir Productions, which we advertised as our "First Film Series Ever." And he's still producing rock'n'roll film nights at various East Village clubs.

I see him often on St. Mark's Place. "It was a great time, Stanley," he said to me recently. "I remember when I was just dreaming and conceptualizing the series, wanting to show the beginnings of rock'n'roll. Then I saw you at the door of Club 57 and I said to myself, 'Will I be doing my films here?' And you just said, 'It's the right place for you. You've got every Monday.'

"I was so proud to start it. I put a lot energy into it and then on a Monday in April, 1978, I started my 'Reelin', Rockin' Film Festival' with Bo Diddley, Little Richard, Chuck Berry and Jerry Lee Lewis. And now it's been over 15 years."

We showed all kinds of films at the club. To the rock films we added the Monster Movie Club, cartoons, and sex-and-violence films from the '60s. Then break dancers and graffiti painters brought in more street art and spirit. From Club 57 they went on to Lincoln Center with "Serious Fun."

So this is how we first kicked the ball. Soon there were many adventurous people to help us to keep running with it.

Chapter Three

The Punks Are Coming

Steve Roxon stood at the bar at the East Village Student Club, 57 St. Mark's Place. The tall, blonde, blue-eyed all-American boy smiled frankly and asked me for a beer. He drank it, looking around, always with a smile on his face. After a while he introduced himself, and then he said, "I like this place but it's not too crowded. Listen to me. If you want I'll talk to my friends, and we'll play in here. Rock music. I'm sure you'll like them, and they'll like you. I'll be back the day after tomorrow; you just think about changing your program."

But he was back the next night to watch the rock'n'roll movie. I tried to give him another beer, saying, "That's OK, it's on the house," but he put the money on the counter. He was too proud to take another beer on the house. In spite of the fact that he often had little money in his pocket, he never would take free drinks. And it was through him and his friends that I grew to like the young rockers of New York.

The winter of 1977-78 was a hard one. The snow piled up on the streets and sidewalks in mountains. You could hardly walk. The first night of Steve's program, I didn't expect to find many people at the club. I came in around 7p.m. to struggle with the snowdrifts. I saw leaflets on the lampposts as I walked through the neighborhood: "Rock Party at Club 57. Free Party with 4 Bands ... The Tears, The Communists, The Blessed and the New York Niggers." When I got to the club there was a huge crowd outside. Instead of the snow, I had to struggle through the crowd just to get inside.

When I did, the first thing I saw was a girl from The Blessed onstage singing. She moved her hands, her legs, her whole body in a movement of free, insouciant expression. She was the first punk singer I ever saw. She was dressed in a short skirt, a blouse that was half-ripped off her, striped socks, and boy's boots. Her hair was messy, but decorated with a ribbon. She acted like an amused little girl. There was only the music and her. She didn't care if anyone else was in the room.

"Hi, Stan," somebody called out to me. It was Steve. He didn't say too much, and neither did I. We just looked at each other and smiled. Finally I said, "It's great, Steve." And I patted his cheek and poked him in the stomach. I don't know why, but at that time I had the habit of patting or squeezing everybody's cheek who had gained my friendship. And I still do it. Some people got a little embarrassed, but I started to feel like the father of all people.

From that night on, a steady stream of punks came to play and hang out at the club. They were from all over—California, South Carolina, Ohio, Queens. There were no bosses. Everybody just did what was needed. My mother, who helped me clean the club, spent many evenings with them. They were hungry, so she started bringing in cheese sandwiches—she found a cheap place for cheese, and for a while it seemed like we were feeding the whole East Village. The kids started calling her Mommy. Around that time we bought a pair of parakeets, and they would fly all over the club. (They were afraid of loud music, though, and we had to put them upstairs.)

Between the bands and the audience, the neighbors were terrorized. I am a sensitive man, but I had to close my heart to the neighbors and open it for these kids. Maybe because I never had kids of my own, I loved these young people as if they were my children. Many of them began to treat me as a surrogate father. The spirit of the time and place had us under a spell, and we moved bravely into an unknown, exciting future.

Each band that night had its own distinct style. Steve's band, The Tears, played at the top of the bill. He played guitar and sang. This mild-mannered boy underwent a personality change onstage, becoming a little villain. He didn't care about anything. He ripped his leather pants. He poured beer on the audience, on his head, into his mouth. Everyone seemed to like it.

Well, not everybody. Steve had plastered posters all around the East Village for the event. This attracted the attention of the Polonia

Club, an organization housed on the second floor of what was then the Yiddish Theater and is now the home of the Village East Cinema. The Polonia Club was connected to the Polish Consulate. Poland was of course under the Communists at the time, and a man from the club came to talk to me before the show. He was quite polite. I had left Poland in 1972, and was never much involved in politics, though I had visited the Polonia Club a few times.

"Mr. Stanley," he said to me, "There is a very bad provocation in your club. There are posters on the street where everyone can see them, advertising a band called The Communists. They will give your club a bad reputation. Take those posters down and cancel the show. That band is very provocative. And the name itself! And those people are very bad, and violent." He looked very serious and angry.

I don't know who sent him. I do know that, when my mother went to Poland some time later, she was investigated by the Polish Secret Police because of her connection with Club 57. It turned out that they knew everything that I had done at the club, and whom I had dealt with.

I answered the man in my best political manner. "Oh yes? I'll take them off the program immediately. I really wasn't sure they were even going to play, and anyway I thought they were called The Socialists. I'm glad you told me that, I really appreciate it very much." He repeated his warnings in closing, using what pressure he could through his connections with the Communist Party, as well as an array of ominous facial expressions. It was a cold blast against freedom of expression, common sense and humor. Big Brother was watching, even here.

Communists, I salute you! You played a great set that night. I don't care if you were communists or anarchists, or just being provocative, you were the best people in the world that night, and you reminded us about freedom in America, which lets us be communists if we want to be.

"The New York Niggers" were a nice bunch of young blacks from various parts of the city. I became good friends with them, especially the leader Leo Faison. They had a huge loft on Greenwich Street, which became famous for the rock'n'roll parties they threw.

Leo had a nobility and dignity about him. I tried to learn from him how to be a gentleman. Sometimes he wore a white tuxedo, which contrasted beautifully with his skin.

They wrote their name all over the club, and soon after a good friend of mine, an English teacher who worked at the church, came into the club very upset.

"I don't believe what I saw at the club! What kind of club is it? What kind of people are coming here? Did you see what they wrote on the walls? Take a look!" He pulled me to the front door in front of the evidence and waited for my response.

I didn't laugh; it was a delicate problem. The teacher was Afro-American and he didn't know the band. I explained to him the irony that was an integral part of the punk movement, and finally we relaxed.

It was a very sociable and intelligent crowd. Their clothing at the time was quite contrary to fashion: Army boots on their feet, ripped stocking and socks. The girls wore very short skirts, or ripped jeans, with many different-colored patches. Stripes were popular, from top to bottom. Safety pins were everywhere, keeping clothing together or hanging from ears or noses. Fashion of the lumpen proletariat of Europe mixed with the French Revolution, plus everything you could invent with your fantasy. If you were in a different mood, you could be elegant. You could wear a short white jacket from your grandpa and a narrow tie around your neck. You can have any controversial decoration or jewelry that represents your idea of life or destruction. You can have a swastika, a picture of Mao Tse Tung, a hammer and sickle, a skull and a cross. You can have a little of it or a lot.

There was of course much fashion taken from the American Indian. The boys put their hair in standing rays on their head, colored them and created various fantastic designs. If your face had that mad rebellious look, you were a star among your friends. But it was best if you were missing some teeth or had a bruised nose or forehead. Even I got the look when some monster, sent by an angry stranger, punched me in the face on the stairs of the church. He broke a tooth, and Susan Hannaford liked it so much that she called a photographer to record it for all time. She never did that before. So you see, to cut a figure in punk society, you have to have the appropriate dental work.

Where did these people come from?

Though punk originated on the Lower East Side, much of its music and style came back to the US from the streets of London, where it became actually bigger among the youth than it was here, probably because the inflation and depression of the mid-'70s was worse there. It became the standard of revolution for frustrated youth. Less violent and less politically motivated here than in the UK, punk was also a reaction against the hippies, which by then was much too mild and had nothing to say about the problems of the time. The punks were more aggressive, independent, creative, and very loyal in their friendships. They had a strong sense of humor, using irony and sarcasm to point out the hypocrisy of modern life.

There were and are many different kinds of individuals and subgroups that either were called or called themselves punks. But I'm talking about the ones who came through Club 57, or hung around the East Village at the time. They didn't care that much about their clothing, they just liked to show their independence. They knew they were abandoned by family, government and society. So in revenge they abandoned society themselves. They looked at others (if they looked at all) as if they were creatures from outer space. They were not jealous if you came here in a stretch limousine to buy cocaine. They accepted spare change to buy pizza and soda, their everyday meal. They lacked good nutrition. But still they were beautiful American kids, children of the street and part of the great spirit of America. Their possessions were a bag, a guitar and a naked mattress in a bare white apartment in Alphabet City. If they got a job, a position and some money, they remained punks in their hearts.

Always the life of comfort will interfere with the freedom of the soul, the expressive mind looking forward with love and friendship at whatever happiness and sorrow life will give, with a heart that misses the lost paradise of childhood, with serious eyes full of the joy of breathing and having the life that fate gives. If you think you are a punk and don't have these experiences and feelings, maybe you are just one-quarter of a punk.

And who is walking the streets here between the punks? Many jealous, rich youths with ripped jeans and iron jewelry. Their parents, their friends, their society didn't give them these feelings of personal freedom, that they can feel like birds flying in the sky, the clouds, close to the sun. Only here can they smell the richness of life, punks' life. The punks' poverty, instead of destroying them, is like a rich soil on which can grow and blossom into the most beautiful flowers in America. The flowers will be the future fruit of this country. Do you have the dream of having an apple for dessert or a pillow under your head? No, you don't. It would be different for you to experience their sensibility. But don't be afraid to come here to St. Mark's Place, which is the safest place in the world in the middle of the night. Do punks use drugs? No more than anybody else. Rich people are the apple of the drug lord's eye. Punks hate to steal when they don't have a job, and they share their slice of pizza when their friend is hungry. But if they steal, whom do we have to blame?

The punk movement was already underway when they started coming to Club 57 in 1978. CBGB was their main nest. Their local idols were Patti Smith, The Ramones, The Contortions, and many others. They loved The Sex Pistols, The Clash and Generation X from England. They liked the British flag, together with skulls, which symbolized their psychic life. This showed their contempt for the consumer lifestyle. Creativity and high spirits made them closer to God and human pride.

Would you say I am taking this too far? But the punks unlocked my feelings, which I had missed my whole life. I got it, and I adore it. You may say I am overly romanticizing this epoch. Maybe according to some psychologist I am. But according to my personality, I am normal. I can appreciate Van Gogh, Chopin and Mozart the same way I like Michael Jackson, Cindy Lauper, Keith Haring and the kid on the street painting the walls and my new love, the music of the Andes Mountain Indians, which came a few years ago to New York streets, with its unusual yearning and nostalgia for lost paradise and the unknown world, which we still have to discover somewhere and sometime in the infinite future. I am how I am.

You can experience the same if you like. Leave hate forever behind you, look with open eyes and heart into other people's hearts. Start to do, and do, and do, anything positive, serve other people and participate in improving the human condition. You don't have to be punk, but you have to have a child's soul. Then you will never be bored, you will be happy and you will get that heartstring, which is missing, and then you can hear clearly the most harmonious songs in your life, the song of your soul. You see? It is very easy if only you wish it.

Come here to St. Mark's Place and maybe you'll meet that strictly punkish Denise Mercedes, the leader of the band The Stimulators. Her band, together with The Invaders, pioneered the opening of Irving Plaza. She always had a very London punk look, with lots of bracelets and chains on black leather clothing. The Stimulators' drummer was Harley, ten years old at the time, who dressed and acted the same as she. Harley eventually started his own band, but then he was considered the "grandson" of Club 57. Denise had the eyes and the restless soul of a Gypsy. She was always ready to fight for the truth, as well as her friends. The personification of the East Village punk scene, Denise probably spent more time at CBGB than in her apartment.

Denise's energy and moral support helped give me the courage to open Club 57 At Irving Plaza. Thus it was only natural that I hired her band to open for the B-52's, the New Wave band from Athens, Georgia that was then on its way to the stardom it still enjoys to this day.

The Stimulators only played with the B-52's one night. After that the B-52's refused to play on the same bill with them. They found the Stimulators' backstage manner too aggressive for them. Denise was upset and frustrated. She couldn't understand how the B-52's could be unhappy with the combative punk attitude that was part of the movement that had created the whole scene. But the B-52's, a very genteel rock band, wasn't interested in playing such games.

I'm glad that soon after, The Stimulators got a recording contract, and presented me with a copy. We had spent many hours talking about music, life, creativity, and what the future had in store. But that hard girl was hurt by the cancellation. It came with a stream of tears and many kicks against the side of the building from her army boots. She had lost her first break. But she hadn't lost my heart, or her spirit. She was everywhere, telling all the bands and the kids about Irving Plaza. "Stan!" she yelled. "I know lots of English bands who'll play for you. They'll love you for it, and you'll make money!"

It was very easy to fall into her state of crazy excitement. I wanted to turn Irving Plaza into a Mother Club for all those bands looking for a home. I started observing them carefully, and found a special joy in watching a young band develop its act, its stage presence. Many had never been onstage before. It was as exciting watching those beginners as it is watching a newborn child. It gave me more satisfaction than watching big bands with their cool professionalism, even if they brought in big bucks.

Those new kids look to you as your big hope, guardian to the door of Heaven. They'll do anything you want for your acceptance, praise and help. And you can't say no. And they give you their sincere gratitude. You know they struggled to buy their expensive instruments, collecting the money any way they could, and that they kissed them the moment they got home from the store. And then they got together in the garage or the basement. They played their music with great love as they love their own family, with the hope that maybe they will someday be as famous as Elvis.

At least they will have a good time celebrating their youth and bonhomie. Can we have a better time of life than when we are teenagers, discovering the world, wanting to help God in His creation? That's what you feel when you are young, as always a new generation looks to a bright future, that bright lamp on the high mountain where everybody is going with his dreams.

The punks created a new style in the music and fashion industries, creating a lot of wealth among business people but very little for themselves. Their unique character and lifestyle enriched and added color to society, in the East Village, in New York, and in many other cities of the world. I have seen people kissing the Pope's ring; I have seen men kissing ladies' hands. But I have also had the experience of my hands being kissed by very hard punk girls in public, which I found embarrassing. It was a very emotional time for me.

They were not the ones who attacked me in front of the club, breaking my tooth. They didn't curse at me or want to murder me. The Punks came to Irving Plaza with their hearts, their work, their ideas and their money. And for this we were punished by the primitive, envious people—these "normal" people who went to church every Sunday.

The punks don't all go to church or temple. But they find the spirit of God in their hearts. In this spirit they share their pizza like the matzoh of the Last Supper. There is a lot of love in that ceremony, and they are very happy after they perform it. Do you have an empty church, Bishop? Try His way. Don't just throw stones at the sinners.

Leave your herd of sheep and look for the one who is lost and in danger on a precipice. Or perhaps you should try the Polish way. In Poland nearly every church service includes rock bands, and the church is filled with teenagers. Sometimes strange ways lead to Him and the truth.

Some churches there resemble Club 57 in the way they open their doors to youth. Perhaps God first visits them in the basement before going on to the "official showroom" upstairs. Do you know why he came to Earth 2,000 years ago? He said himself he came to change some rules that don't apply to the development of humanity. And hypocrisy always creeps into one's house and has to be thrown out with the garbage.

This chapter is about the punks, but perhaps it has turned into a philosophical treatise: Stanley's Philosophy about Dealing with Youth. It's quite simple, really. You must have love for people.

The kids came to me and said, "We want to be with you." And they gave me their hearts and eyes to see and feel through them that secret tunnel of bright light that leads just inches from Heaven. But it was only a temporary state. Maybe that's why Club 57 ceased to exist, to give others a chance to look for truth.

Perhaps this chapter is too spiritual in focus. But art cannot exist without the spirit.

Maybe it is good to live longer, but I tell you it is better to live shorter and well than longer and bad. The punks from the East village made my personality, and indeed my whole life, much richer than ever before.

Chapter Four

The Invaders

July 12, 1994. The summer is truly hot and humid, and as the saying goes "even the eldest do not remember such heat." I have just come back from the cool countries of Scandinavia, straight into this fever. I return to the old habits that make up my well-organized timetable: swimming pool, Metropolitan Museum, and my domestic economy day, Tuesday.

Yes, every Tuesday I go to the bank on the corner of Second Avenue and St. Mark's Place, and then I have lunch at The Zen Café, the Japanese restaurant between Second and Third Avenues. A Buddha greets me in the window, and a crane with a long beak overlooks my table. And it's always at 1 p.m. Sometimes my friends come to see me there. Today someone has come to see me, too.

My friend Earl opens the door to the bank on the corner for me, as usual. I don't have any objections to tipping him: He earns his money instead of begging for it. I smile at him and he smiles back. He knows that I like his service. His smile is sincere. And this brilliant day is more radiant because of his smile.

An undisciplined, light-hearted New Yorker, I try to cross an equally undisciplined street against the lights. For so many years now I have been tramping these streets of the East Village that it doesn't even cross my mind that I am doing something wrong; I feel like I am in my own house.

I suddenly make a stop. A small crowd of people and a police barrier block my entrance to the Zen Café. An entire block is barred. There is a crime scene in the store where they say they sell punk accessories.

Drugs? It is common to find a crime scene here and I don't pay much attention to it, but I must find another way to my piece of marinated fish, and my brown rice, but most of all the green tea called Yama Motoyama. All my friends who ever passed through Zen can't stand Yama Motoyama, but I feel great after drinking it, and I don't much mind the way it tastes.

"Hey, Stanley, how are you!" Someone calls out to me and taps me on the shoulder and in a moment I am embracing Gregor. Gregor's smile brightens up my day even more than Earl the Doorman's, and now the day can't possibly be any brighter. This embrace tells both of us that it feels so good to meet again. Gregor can't get through, either, although he lives on the block.

We decide have lunch together at Veselka, a Ukrainian place on Ninth Street and Second Avenue.

Gregor is happy today, and to me he looks like he is twenty years old. Yet we met fifteen years ago. When we saw each other then, he would always have the same kind, French-American punk eyes that told me our friendship was a historical one, a great experience.

During lunch, Gregor's expression suddenly becomes serious. "You know," he says, "we are having a concert at the Bottom Line this Thursday in memory of Bruce Pascow. You knew him. He passed away a few months ago from AIDS. He was a good guy, but like many of us, he was involved in the East Village life, and he paid the price.

"You will be on the guest list. I hope you will come. Peter will come from Boston, he lives there with his wife and children, and Finn will be there, too. We'll have a few bands and some actors will perform, people involved in the artistic life of the East Village."

And so I am here at the Bottom Line. The three surviving members of the Invaders greet me warmly. I listen to poets, I listen to musicians, I listen to the memories about a boy whom the cruel lady, the Angel of Death, took away from us, I listen to the silence of the concert participants and to the shouting secret, the reason for this evening's gathering, emanating from the music: the curse of AIDS.

Once again I recall the time during which I first met the Invaders. As soon as they saw Club 57 they wanted to play there. The club wasn't decorated at all and they liked it—they liked that it lacked the atmosphere of a "business." They especially liked the fact that there were no chairs! But mainly, I think that when one is young and when one loves life and music, and when one has aspirations, it is good to play everywhere as much as you can. And Club 57 was the place to be.

Five laughing pusses and ten sparkling eyes were fixed on me. I thought that these five "Invaders" were more like angels. These are the people that were called punks. I would never have the heart to refuse them.

Gregor Laraque, the band's leader, was a guitarist and vocalist. Born in Haiti, he had a French background. "When I was young," he said in an interview in the New York Rocker, "On weekends I used to come to the Village in New York. Then I would walk around and I would say to myself, "This is where I want to be.""

"I used to come to the Village, too," said the drummer Finn Hunt in the same interview, "and every guy I would see walking with a guitar, I would ask, 'What band are you with, where d'ya play?'" He wanted to be called Finn Fun, but the rest of the band said that he had to earn it.

Bruce Pascow, guitar and vocals, grew up in New Jersey. "It was so boring there you had to learn how to play something, just to have something to do."

And Johnny Ian, the baby of the band and a saxophonist, added, "I was born in New York Hospital. I've lived all my life on this fucking rock. I've played since I was fourteen. I've played everything."

"Gregory," I said back then, "if you are not going to play for me this year, then we are worth nothing." I am not sure what else we said then and later, but we turned everything into humor. Sometimes I would like to return to these times of unrestrained thoughts, speech and actions.

"You know that I like all New Wave music," I said to Gregory, "but you also know that this is loud music. Look at what it says on the lampposts." I showed him a flyer which I had torn from a post, protesting Club 57's noisy band nights.

And there were plenty of such flyers. I constantly had meetings with police and I trod such a path to the courts so that Centre Street should be named after me. But I wasn't very surprised, people want to sleep, after all, and it's not their concern that the YMCA and other such organizations do not provide enough places for youth to allow them to participate in creating our new American culture and art. And the police care only for the drug dealers to have a place to deal so they can get their share.

Do the church or other religious institutions worry about youth? O yes, Baker and Swaggart especially. Yet the elders love them very much and give them lots of money, at least more than they give to the Guardian Angels. If you want to know how I feel about the young, listen to this verse from the poem of Adam Mickiewicz:

Here, heartless, spiritless, throng skeletons in sorry plight!
Youth, give me wings, that I may rise
Above this dead world, curs't and bare
Into the realm of dreams and light
For ardor brings forth marvels there
Strews each new dream with blossoms rare
And dresses each in golden hope's fair guise.

This is why I said to Gregor, "I kindly invite you to participate in the opening of a new place at Irving Plaza, Seventeen Irving Place. I want to 'invade' this place with you, O.K.?"

"Oh, yes!" all answered. It was not only a consent, it was also a call to invasion. The next day we all met at the old Polish National Home.

This is how, in two weeks, we opened Club 57 at Irving Plaza. The whole show was organized by Gregor and his band, including posters, sound, lights, and even booking LaPeste, the Stimulators, der Cuban Heels and other bands.

"As soon as I see this stage it's an instant love affair. So I started helping him book bands there and we booked ourselves into there a lot," said Gregory in the same interview with the New York Rocker.

"As further proof of how unfashionable these guys are," stated the writer, "note that they were the pioneers of what was once New York's most un-trendy club, the Irving Plaza."

Friday, July 14, 1978: The crowd wasn't big, but we had lots of fun, some people smoked pot, we lost three hundred dollars, and we had an argument with the owners of Irving Plaza, because they had to clean the hall although we paid one of their people to do it. And soon after we all became good friends.

The news about the Club 57 went around. Bands came, bands played, and we grew. Gregory always placed posters around town. One time, on the wall of Klein's, the old department store at Union Square, they placed the largest poster I ever saw, with just their name on it. From then on I called them "the largest poster in New York."

As we worked together, we spent plenty of time drinking Buds, talking about our bright futures, about bands making their own records, and about all our good times together. They believed in me, and I believed in them. Except that we didn't know yet that behind every good will a devil stands who wants to destroy the dreams people have. It happened later to us. Now we know that even if our future didn't end happily, the whole experience was a great lesson and an adventure.

On Saturday, September 20, 1980, Club 57 organized an Award Night. That evening Regina Richards and the Red Hots played, along with Gregory's girlfriend Michelle. Blondie appeared as a guest. It was an interesting evening and to make it even more interesting I asked the Invaders to bartend and serve drinks. They spilled half the alcohol on the bar. Every drink was straight up. I am not even sure if they charged for the drinks. I had my eyes on them, for it looked as if they would finish every drop this way. Fortunately it was only for 15 minutes. And the award, a well-earned award, of course, the Club 57 Gold Eagle, went to the Invaders. Here are excerpts from the speech I gave, which I somehow held onto all these years:

"Several years ago, only two rock clubs existed, Max's and CBGB. We would like to salute these clubs for their great contribution of creating an atmosphere of free artistic expression, and shaping new music as we know it today. Over two years ago when Club 57 first opened its doors, there were many bands with no place to play. With the urging and help of these bands, we opened 'Irving Plaza' for rock dance parties, which was something new at the time ... But we could not have done it without the help and optimism of the Invaders and their leader, Gregor Laraque.

"In this hall we have had many great and famous American entertainers. Some of their managers have forgotten about our club, and forgotten that money isn't everything. Now the biggest support we have is from English bands and from a great humanitarian and friend, Ian Copeland. Another friend of Club 57 is David Johansen, who, with his great concern for the club and its public, understands that friendship is more important than money. Now perhaps all of you will understand why the first Club 57 Award is not being given to Elvis Costello or John Lydon, but to Gregor Laraque, a good East Village kid who first opened this Club 57 and still offers help when we need him. Of course, we also remember his friends, Peter, Bruce, Finn and John, who together invaded this club, the music scene, and our hearts. The invasion is complete, the war is over, and New York has the best rock club in the world."

And so I am here, at the Bottom Line, thinking about you, Bruce. You were with us; with the Invaders, you worked, you played, and you rejoiced with us. Perhaps it was you who somehow brought me here tonight, to the Bottom Line, so that I may not forget what's best in one's life: youth, enthusiasm, work, friendship, one's love towards good things, and music. I listened to your music then, and I hear your music now. This was the music of your heart and of your soul. That's why I am here, and I feel such sorrow. I always thought that you, like everyone else, played only for me. I would forget that hundreds of other people surrounded me.

You boys once wrote a song called "Such a Romantic." But I think that it is you who are the most romantic boys in the world.

Chapter Five

New Wave Vaudeville

The Pharaoh arrives on his litter, wearing a gold crown and matching skirt, carried by four servants dressed in loincloths. A wide, jewel-encrusted collar adorns his skinny neck, while in his hands he holds the symbols of Upper and Lower Egypt. He smiles joyfully at the triumphal music. On his feet are black tap shoes.

David McDermott, the East Village's newest vaudeville star, steps down from his litter and smiles at his friend Kristian Hoffman, whose band is about to launch into an accompaniment of David's song, "King of the Nile," which David has written for the occasion.

It was a good way to open New Wave Vaudeville, a very important event in East Village New Wave culture, and David was the star of the show. He sang several more numbers and took on different personalities, which was easy for him, an eccentric young man known as a painter, thespian and 1920s-era dandy. With his companion Walter Fleming, and later Peter McGough, David created his own world of glamour in Alphabet City, making it seem more like the Bohemia of Paris in the 19ᵗʰ Century than the broken-down ghetto it was for most people.

"I am the greatest! I am history!" David's voice carried all the way to the bar in the very back of Irving Plaza. David was true to history, because in the Metropolitan Museum of art at that time—November 1978—was a traveling exhibition of the treasures of King Tutankhamun's tomb. And just as in the 1920s, when the tomb was first discovered, David used its inspiration to liven up the contemporary culture. To drive the point home, David rented an old Rolls-Royce to drive around town and screamed at people to see the show.

New Wave Vaudeville was the invention of three energetic young people: producers Tom Scully, a new graduate of the School of Visual Arts, and his girlfriend Susan Hannaford; and director Ann Magnuson, an actress who had recently arrived in the city from West Virginia.

The three, who had not yet begun to work with me at Club 57, searched the city for talent. What they found was a Pandora's Box of performing artists, including a fire-eater in S&M clothing, punk fashion designers Tish & Snooky Bellamo doing a comedy-song-and-dance routine, and clothing designer Animal X playing punk music and smashing her pink guitar.

Then there was that classic, tragic couple, the punk jazz artist James Chance (a/k/a James White) and Anya Philips, who staged a "Dating Game"-type competition, which was won by Lydia Lunch.

Another star of the show was Beanie, the singing dog. If you ever played harmonica near a dog, you know that the dog will start crying, and Beanie, a collie, was no exception, except Beanie was onstage, and he had a very good stage presence.

But I really loved the very classy striptease performed by Lady Bug, a young classical dancer who performed with a hand puppet to the Carpenters' "Close To You," displaying a number of graceful ballet moves and a very limber body.

I didn't like everything, though. Watching the rehearsal from the balcony, I called Susan over and told her:

"You are great people and I admire you. But there a few points in the performance I really don't like. One is Tish & Snooky's joke about the Polish Pope. They are saying that he was chosen only because nobody else was available. But there are two ways to look at it. Maybe it was because there are no more smart Italians anymore. Or maybe John Paul is great because he is Polish, and the world can always count on the Poles if there is any problem. Like when Copernicus published his book about the Earth moving around the Sun, or when Marie Curie-Sklodowska discovered the Rad and Polon, or when two Polish generals, Kosciusko and Pulaski came to America to help General Washington win the war and achieve freedom for America."

"Oh, Stan, that's OK, we can cancel it," said Susan, "even if the joke was first made by Russell Wolinski."

The joke was never canceled, but I wasn't too hard on them. I had to get used to the American sense of humor. But I think I was right.

Didn't the Poles invent the "solidarity" movement, which, together with the Polish Pope, helped to bring down Communism? And look here in the United States. Isn't it Polish Spring mineral water that helps the American people quench their thirst? Ha ha!

There was one other thing.

"Susan," I began again, "I believe Kristian is the nicest man of all the performers. And I am as frustrated as he is with the government officials, the churches and hypocritical society. But I disagree with him throwing the cross on the stage floor during his rebellious performance, as I disagree with burning the American flag."

"Are you going to cancel our show, Mr. Censor?" she replied.

I felt hate in her voice and I could see it in her eyes.

It is not easy to be hard on a person whom one likes. But I pressed on.

"I learned the hard way that even for very liberal things there is a limit," I answered.

Susan left the balcony. A cold spirit came up between us. I have never been sure how much of this coldness remained in her heart, even though she told me many times, later, "Stanley, we love you and you know it."

Of course, I didn't take any money from the door, except for a few hundred dollars for electricity and cleaning. When all the shows were over she came over again.

"Stanley, we would like to have a party with the artists. We didn't make any extra money. Could you help us?"

"Here is 300 bucks. Is that enough?"

"Thanks!" She jumped on my neck like a daughter and gave me a big kiss. Ann and Tom came up to me too. "We didn't know you before, Stan. May we invite you to the party?"

"No, I can't go. I have volunteer work to do. I have been organizing the New York Society of the Friends of the Health Center for Children in Poland. I hope my project with Club 57 and Irving Plaza will help too, when it comes to funding. And I know what I'm doing with great kids like you."

Those kids came to me in a few days and said, "We were lost in New York, but we found you. Can we work with you, Stan?"

"You were my dream, my whole life," I answered. I was at the right place at the right time. Could I be with the right people too?

"Who is that man with the beard, Stan?"

"This is my new manager, Alex."

"Can you trust him?"

"I have nobody excellent now. He speaks English and Polish, so I think he will be good for solving problems with the Polish speaking people at Irving."

The young man, who was about 30 then, came up to us and said to Susan and Tom, "I heard that you'd like to work with Stanley's Club 57."

"Yes," replied Tom, "We'd like to, if possible."

"He is the best man I've met in New York," the young man said. "He took me for his manager. He threw a birthday party for me at the club. I never had such a party, and so many good friends, in my life. I am so happy. I will pay him back for this, and for his trust in me. You made a good choice to work with him. All the East Village kids love him very much."

"Okay, Alex," I said. "That's enough. Goodbye, and leave me alone."

The trio of Tom, Susan and Ann was welcomed at the club. I moved Chris Gremski to Irving Plaza to work with Alex, and made Ann the manager of Club 57 at St. Mark's Place. And the new era of the club began.

As I stood again on the balcony watching the rehearsal, my heart was leaping and I thought, "Wow! I fell in love with them and I got them!"

Then came the last big pillar of the show: Klaus Nomi.

Klaus Sperber was the performer's real name, and his performance was a tremendous hit. Klaus came from Germany and worked in a pastry shop at the World Trade Center, and was lonely like everyone else who came here. He attended the various punk and new wave clubs in the city, including Max's and CBGB.

Klaus's trump cards were his voice, which spanned several octaves, and his unusual personality, appearance (he had pointed ears and nose) and sense of style. He called his performance "Nomi" and was later known by that name.

For this piece he made his face and hands white like snow, painted his lips a deep red, and wore a devilish black costume. He appeared out of a cloud of smoke onstage and sang an aria from Wagner's opera, "Sampson And Delila," in a full soprano voice. He seemed to be a creature from another planet, and after he sang he disappeared slowly into the smoke the same way he came, with a stony face and sad eyes, like a spirit who visited Earth without hope of staying because it wasn't his world.

With his high forehead you could imagine he had a great, strange intelligence, and in fact he was a new breed of artist who started a new era of horror and expression of life somewhere beyond heaven, beyond many galaxies. Where are you now, Klaus? Did you find that world beyond that you were showing us? Are you coming some quiet night to the East Village, over its streets and houses? Do you miss us as we miss you?

Having Klaus in the New Wave Vaudeville show sated my desire to capture the best of New York's New Wave at the end of the '70s.

I was going to the top.

Chapter Six

The Monster Movie Club

Today my wife Grace and I went to Central Park to get tickets for Shakespeare's "Two Gentlemen of Verona" at the Delacorte Theater. The play was canceled, so instead we took a walk to Cleopatra's Needle, and then over to the statue of King Jagiello, just opposite the small pond by the Theater. Here, every Sunday people meet to dance European folk dances. Then we crossed the park to the Angel's fountain, and then the Wollman Rink to observe the dancing skaters. As more skaters whisked by on the footpaths, we went along the Boat Pond, near to where the statue of Hans Christian Andersen reads his stories to bronze children and ducks. We've already passed the statue of Alice in Wonderland.

Finally Grace puts a stop to our wanderings, demanding, "Didn't you promise we'd take a rest near the pond?"

"Oh, yes, sure," I reply. So we come back and sit on a bench bordering the pond, watching the miniature sailboats and tall ships sail to and fro.

Somewhere on the East Side of Manhattan lives Susan Hannaford with her two children, Margaret and Charles.

"You know, Grace, I have to visit Susan and the kids. I miss them. I haven't seen them for a few months now."

My wife starts eating her peach yogurt. I start reading my book, but I keep looking up, looking around. "Go Tuesday," my wife answers.

Is that Susan walking on the other side of the pond? No, it can't be. "Isn't that Susan?" I ask Grace.

"No, that isn't Susan, that's a young girl."

I don't know what's happening with my vision. I'm getting confused.

The young girl is slowly walking toward us. Her head is turned to the side; she is watching something. What is she watching? Two kids.

"Susan!" I yell. The girl moves her head. It looks like her.

"Wow! Stanley!"

Now I know that miracles can happen, at least small ones. I run to her and we hug. And the kids call my name.

We spend this evening in Central Park recalling our past, as usual. And we agree to meet next Tuesday and see "Two Gentlemen of Verona" together. Next Tuesday we meet as planned, and spend more time reminiscing.

Susan was my associate director at Club 57. And she was one of the three who organized the legendary New Wave Vaudeville show in 1978. But above all, she was and is the best friend I ever had.

Susan ran the Monster Movie Club, a weekly series of mostly B-grade horror films from the '50s and '60s. These films enjoyed a renewed popularity among the punk generation, with their exploration of nature and humanity's dark side, now viewed lightheartedly from the vantage point of a more jaded era.

I took her to Club 57, and to my heart, from the first moment I saw her. She knew how to get the best room in that big hotel.

In her heart she was still a kid. I realize now how hungry we, all of us at the club, were for our lost childhood, and we wanted to extend it and be children as long as we could.

Maybe that's why I still like to watch cartoons, especially Tom and Jerry, and Susan, together with Tom, created the Monster Movie Club, which dealt with life and death from the perspective of outlandishness. For every screening Susan dressed herself in the style of Morticia from the Addams Family, which was not hard for her to do: She has more than a slight resemblance to that character, with the addition of very large and haunting dark brown eyes.

Susan and Tom had very good taste, and served all the greats: "The Birds," "Cat Women of the Moon," "King Kong," "The Spider," "The Horror of the Beach," "I Was A Teenage Werewolf," "The Mummy's Tomb," et cetera.

Once I visited them in their home in a Chrystie Street loft. It was a scary looking old building, filled mostly with Chinese garment factories, a perfect setting for the hosts of the Monster Movie Club. It was evening, and the neighborhood was spooky—exactly the kind of area I don't go to after dark.

I don't even know how I got there. A ramshackle elevator brought me to the top floor, passing lofts where Asian men and women, probably all immigrants, labored over sewing machines. I saw table after table topped with mountains of fabrics and partially-made clothing. It had a unique smell about it.

Susan and Tom's loft was quite different. The living room was large enough for a good dance party. The ceiling and walls were stamped tin painted white, while the doors, floors and window trim were green. Abstract paintings, horror show memorabilia and a real stuffed bear's head comprised the decorative element. As the central heat was scanty, they had put in a coal-fired stove. Nearly wall-to-wall windows gave a stunning view of the city, with so many stars at night, it felt like they were going to burst inside of the loft. Two dogs shared the space as well, wire-haired terriers named Rio and Tip. The dogs quickly made off with my shoes, but came back to jump all over my pants, at which they did not desist, making it impossible to drink my coffee.

Susan lit some candles, but the big room was still mostly dark. Tom smoked his Camels and the cigarette tip glowed like a jack o'lantern, leaving a tracer of red light from his mouth to the ashtray. I didn't see any crystal ball, but I did see two cats lurking about as if there was one there to curl around. The black one, named Kathy, lay on the sofa, occasionally getting up to walk between the dogs very confidently. Lucy, the orange cat, had provocative eyes that flashed in that dark room, but she was shy and kept her distance, perched high up on the loft bed.

Through the bribe of dog biscuits, I was able both to save my pants and drink my coffee, while we discussed the possibility of the existence of a ghost living in the building. After this we went to the roof garden. You may know some of these downtown roof gardens. They are not like those on Park Avenue, but much more romantic and comfortable. You can do anything you want to here on the black tar roof, just be careful not to step out too far, or you'll end up in the alley in a hurry, where no one will find you. In wooden beds were a profusion of flowers, including bushes full of roses. Two chairs and a table filled one corner: on the other side, attached to the chimney, was a movie screen. Tom brought out a projector and we watched a monster movie, though I'm sure I can't remember which one it was.

That was 15 years ago, and I never returned to their loft, not because I was afraid, but because things became so busy at Club 57 and in the rest of my life. I just wonder why, whenever something is very special, romantic and close to your heart, and you meet the right kind of people whose company you enjoy, the time is so terribly short. You discover with them new worlds, new adventures, new beginnings, and then everything fades into the past so quickly. And you miss them.

We did many things that never come to our heads now. Something was boiling in our brains. We wanted to be a part of the crazy rush of the 20th century. We wanted to attach ourselves to the stream of its appetite, desires, aspirations, ideas. We wanted to be seen, and to be distinguished among our friends and in society. For this Tom ran around New York for new ideas, for new blood, you could say.

Before each film he gave a very instructive speech. You'd never know from his appearance and demeanor that he was the head of the Horror Movie Party. Outside his involvement with the films, his life was markedly devoid of bloodshed. In fact, in my opinion Tom Scully was always the Number One American Gentleman, calm, genial and humble. Always soft-spoken, always loath to cause his fellow human being any pain. Any problems of his own he bore with great patience. His presence I found greatly aided my own psychological state. I was happy to consider him as one of my close friends, to my circle, one whom I will miss for the rest of my days.

But even as I describe this person as remarkably well-balanced, let me stress that his head was a boiling pot of dreams and passions. Tom, for me you were always such a wise man, that I will never understand how you and Susan did not stay together. Later, in your frustration, you went to Paris to become part of the American New Wave that the French were so eager to know. We never saw you again. I don't know why. But I am always with you. Someday your children will know what a wonderful man their father was.

Tom always liked to read into my expressions. When I was worried he called me Stanley Stress. So you know there was a lot to worry about. But I was already worried about losing you, Tom. I worried that one day I would lose you and all the other kids who gave me so much love and friendship.

But I also want to show your amusing side. So let's look at the biggest night of the year for the Monster Movie Club: Halloween.

It was two weeks to Halloween, 1980, when Tom Scully gave the following speech: "Dear monsters: In two weeks our club is organizing a party in a real cemetery in Manhattan. There is an old cemetery on Second Street between First and Second Avenues. It is called the Marble Cemetery and it was founded in 1831. In it is the tomb of James Lenox, founder of the New York Public Library, as well as those of several other dignitaries. According to latest reports, every year ghosts from all over Manhattan have a great ball. It is our ambition to attend as witnesses and participants at so great a social event. But so as not to disturb the ball, we will meet at 11 p.m., first to do an inspection and take pictures to prove our bravery and good connections with the afterworld. To make sure they won't recognize us as living creatures, we have to change into different kinds of beings. At midnight we'll come out of our hiding places and we'll join the party."

Suddenly the light went off in the club, and many squeals, groans and awful sounds were heard. Then the lights came on again, and Tom was on the floor struggling with the legendary Sampson. Then I saw Mark holding his girlfriend, saying, "Don't be afraid. I saw Drew turn the light off. And those groans were special effects made by John, Ann and Susan, from behind the bar." But Tom heard this slander, and refuted it quite strenuously.

At the same time he worked to put the members at ease, telling them, "Don't worry. Very often ghosts visit our club, but 'til now I kept it secret. We always light candles in here and they behave themselves. But tonight we forgot to light the candles." Then he brought out a huge candelabra that he proceeded to light with five big candles from the church upstairs, which we borrowed without any hope of being able to replace.

The rest of the evening was quiet. In closing, Tom said with dignity, "The whole evening I was watching the room, and I assure you, nothing that occurred was a swindle or a trick. Sometimes people don't believe in ghosts. But do we believe in them? Yes or no?" He raised his voice almost like Jimmy Swaggart. And the members of the congregation answered back in one voice, "YES"!" In fact, they were shocked and disappointed at Mark's earlier display of disbelief.

Mark was reprimanded for his remarks, and he repented and was forgiven. But he did have to sweep the floor of the club for his bad manners.

Two weeks later at the appointed hour everyone gathered at the cemetery gate. Clever Susan had gotten a permit and key from the city. The pictures were taken, every spot was checked, and John gathered up dead leaves in a big trash bag. But it wouldn't be John if he didn't pull some kind of prank. He added stones to one of the bags to weigh it down, then got Drew to carry it. Everyone awaited midnight with trembling hearts. I didn't go to the cemetery. I was afraid to get my teeth broken again by some ghost.

But I am telling you that I heard everything from trusted and reliable eyewitnesses that the ball was a great success. Everyone was met by ghosts of distinguished citizens and dignitaries of New York. Also invited were witches, hags, vixens, wizards, incubi, succubi, goblins and boogeymen. Even horror movie producers could not have dreamed of this. Some were so terrifying that they scared a few of their fellow creatures, but not us, the living. We showed our bravery and we survived, aided by our disguises. Even when the air conditioner broke and the sultriness became unbearable, people remained. Tom offered the explanation that the ghosts, discovering our deceitful invasion of the cemetery, smelling the leaves we took with us to use in future events, had taken revenge by jinxing the air conditioning system. But the members were not discouraged as a result of these rare occurrences ... though some ghosts have been spotted, disguised in our members' clothing.

Tom's bravery grew as a result of this daring escapade, and he began appearing each week in the costume of a character from the night's film, flaunting his connection to the other world.

And this is the absolute truth, and no one should ever doubt it and try to say it didn't happen just like I said. Many members of the club are still alive, and can confirm it without as much as a wink of the eye.

Now we move to a bigger arena: The Great Halloween party of

Club 57 At Irving Plaza, 1980. All the regular Club 57 members, led by the Monster Movie Club echelon, were dressed to the teeth that evening. Tom and Susan, as the leaders, were very excited. It was their dream event, the culmination of a year's work. They had been waiting for a moment like this to show the world the greatness of the Monster Movie Club. And Irving Plaza was the perfect venue. The staircase and lobby, with its crystal chandelier, looked just like an old palace. Upstairs in the hall were two other huge chandeliers, which were perfect after we changed the regular bulbs with blinking candle-like ones. Tom went crazy with the professional spider web-making gun. Even the toilets did not escape his attentions. We replaced all the regular lights with black lights. We raided the church and brought over all the candlesticks and candelabras we could find. To this we added fake skeletons and portraits of the characters from the Addams Family.

The balcony belonged to Ann. She and her goblin helpers created an entire cemetery, complete with monuments, graves, coffins, bones, fake blood and real dead leaves. These were the leaves we captured from the real cemetery on Second Street, to make the ghouls feel at home. Now it is no longer a joke. It's a real party with our ancestors. Now the coffins: out of one stretches a hand. Out of another, a body is rising by itself. Only the initiated know it is Ann herself. She is all in white, with a veil over her face. Her face and hair are heavily powdered in a deathly white. Her lips are black. When she opens her mouth you can see her long sharp teeth.

The other girls are dancing about like nymphs. Ann demands food and blood-red wine. Then she gets up and stalks the cemetery to the rhythms of DJ Behold. The Siamese Brothers, John Sex and his best friend Shawn McQuate sneakily try to cross the cemetery. They are bound together by the sweater that they wear jointly. But Ann catches up to them, grabs them like a gale wind and strikes them down near her open grave. The wine is already going to their heads.

The nymphs and witches are egging her on with shrieks and laughter.

"Help!" the boys yell. "She wants to rape us!" Ann sits on them and pours wine into their mouths. The party is in full swing now. A horror movie playing on a large screen is showing lots of blood and gore.

Susan is in her usual Morticia-like costume, a long black gown finishing in octopus tails, but even longer than it was in the TV show. Fighting with the tail, she sweeps between ghosts, tables and, of course, she has to walk with full dignity on that palace stairway. She is the mistress of ceremonies, after all. Tom is everywhere at once, working extra-hard to make sure that this event will take its place in the history of our city.

At the bar they are selling bloody marys, of course, and also another one called the "Monster" which is just a few kinds of liquors, juices, salt and pepper, and is half price, but few of the customers are brave enough to try it.

The public has filled up the hall and spills into the lobby. There are bishops and nuns, doctors and mental patients. A few of the patients are completely wrapped in bandages, and some have blood seeping through. Apparently they have just escaped from the hospital. Either that or they're mummies. There's a man who has lost his head, and devils are dancing with angels. Also the President, nearly naked, bearing a sign that read, "I am not a hypocrite. Anybody who believes me can have a dollar."

Many animals have come tonight. Chickens, pigs, some domestic and some wild. There's a skeleton man, a robot, several creatures, and a handful of Frankenstein monsters, each one unique according to the inventiveness and imagination of its maker. There is a cube man and a tree man, a few sheiks from Arabia, and of course several drag queens.

I didn't have a good costume. I had to be a little serious. So I wore my ripped jeans and sneakers and a black shirt. But Susan decided that I wasn't sufficiently outfitted. She blackened one of my eyes and put some bloody slashes on my cheek. She didn't black out a tooth, though, saying "Your broken tooth is good enough."

At midnight the lights went off and a thrill went through the crowd. Suddenly a spotlight burst upon the stage, and our friends The Misfits started playing monster music. Then, from the ceiling came 500 black and white balloons that drifted down upon the gathering. The crowd went crazy. Which was just what Tom and Susan wanted.

Chapter Seven

The Alabaster Girl

"Stanley? Stanley?" I hear a voice. So I am already here, the afterworld. I have already said goodbye to the world of the living and gone under the knife. A quadruple bypass. It was either this or nothing. And I didn't make it. Why don't I feel the fire? Well, it's not so bad after all. Somebody is calling me. I open my eyes a little. I can see some kind of angel.

"Stanley, it's me," the angel says. She looks very familiar to me. She is smiling. "Stanley, how do you feel? It's me, Ann."

I look around. I am still on Earth. "Is it true? Can I see you?" I open my eyes wide. It is good to see her again. "How did you know I was here? Aren't you a long way from Hollywood?"

And she answers, "To see you, Hollywood is plenty close."

* * *

Ann Magnuson, the manager of Club 57 in its early years, has always been a straightforward, natural-mannered girl. At the same time she had the enthusiasm, the energy and the stamina to take the crazy brilliance of the club and the ideas of its members and turn them into things that really happened.

The first thing she did was organize the Ladies' Auxiliary: the conference of the club's young ladies who were just becoming ladies. There they discussed life, art, work, the future, fashion, the club's programming, and the boys, the main subject regarding the latter being, What to do with them?

"The boys will have to be used for many projects," Ann said.

"They're just fooling around looking for trouble, fun and good times. Let's use our charm, show them that we love them, but only if they help us to create our small society, and turn it into the fulfillment of our life's needs.

"We are the future and the beauty of America. We are their companions. We'll be the mothers of their children and guardians of their families. We'll fight with them to make America better, and we'll stand proudly for our country and the Stars And Stripes. Who wants to fight for justice here? Who is brave enough? Are you boys with us?"

And the boys went with them, led by Ann. All of them, from ages 17 to 30. Black and white. Jews, Catholics, Protestants and Atheists, various sex orientations, the gifted and the simpleminded, the artists and the consumers, the musicians, poets and beer-drinkers, the small and the tall, the underpaid, the overeducated, all with heads bursting with dreams, eager to see how far they could go, with Ann at the helm.

* * *

Tonight the club is closed. Some boys and girls are on Club Renovation detail, really just painting and rearranging things. The screen between the entrance and the club has been removed to make more room. The walls are getting a new coat of paint. The low ceiling will be painted black to give it the illusion of greater height. The fluorescent lights are being replaced with several small spotlights. The basement is being turned into a dressing room. The bar gets a psychedelic black paint job. There's no money for new furniture, but as John Sex notes, our club has the comforts of well-broken-in chairs, though he often grumbles about his duty as repairman for those that are just plain broken. We never replaced the chairs. But we started to appreciate their broken-in brokenness. It was like the people—often you get more help from the poor ones.

* * *

July 27th, 1978: The old St. Mark's church-in-the-Bouwerie is burning. Fire is taking its roof, its splendid stained glass windows. I am standing on the corner looking at the flames, feeling the heat on my cheeks. I felt as if my ideas, my work, my life were burning. It happens many times. I have learned the hard way how to stand it, how to lose.

The St. Mark's Church was a sanctuary for many young artists, especially the poets. The fire at the Church, one of the city's irreplaceable treasures, was a tragedy we all felt. During the years it took to rebuild it, the poets had lost their home.

So they arrived at Club 57 to meet and hold readings, with their empty pockets and bad fashion sense. Ann complained to me, "You know they have no money. All they have is their imagination. They're always looking for someone to help them out. How can we support them when we're no better off?"

All we can do is work to make a place for them to be poets. All we get is the gratification that we are a part of their poems, and feel the weird bond that attaches us to them. And we decide to charge them to pay $20 per night for electricity and floor wax, which we use a lot of.

The readings went on for many months. Even Ann, who is not too sentimental, absorbed some of the spirit of nobility from the poems of a new generation of writers. But tonight there is one small problem. Ann comes up to me with the bad news.

"Stanley, what are we going to do with them? They can't even pay us the $20 we agreed on. I skipped lunch today to buy toilet paper for the club!"

I take a piece of paper, write "$20" on it. "Here. Now you have it." She looks at me hard, her lips pressed together. She looks at the people in the room. Then she looks at me again. And she takes the piece of paper.

* * *

Ann has such delicate hands, such fine white skin, but it doesn't keep her from dragging around cases of liquor, tables and chairs, or hammering nails into the wall for exhibitions, or cleaning the club and pushing shut the heavy iron gate.

I saw tears in Ann's eyes more than once. I made believe I didn't. I couldn't afford too. But underneath her delicacy she was hard, stubborn and brave, and quick to forget the problems—those of the club, and those of being its chief scientist.

* * *

I am on the island of Rhodes with my mother in May of 1979. We are admiring the "Alabaster Venus" from Greece's classical period. The alabaster is so delicate and translucent. And I say to my mother, "Aren't you reminded of Ann? Her complexion, her hands and arms?"

My mother looks at the statue, and it seems to speak to her: "Touch me, feel me, admire me, like the sculptor's hands that polished my body and made me from formless stone."

Though we can fondle her only in our imagination, her gentleness touches us, and my mother says, "The alabaster gives her such gentleness, she is really like our Ann." From that time on we refer to Ann as the Alabaster Girl.

* * *

"The Social Event of the Season," the poster announces. "Debutante Ball. Introducing 'The Action Combo' with special Escort Date Kristian Hoffman. May 3rd 1979."

Tonight the girls will show their beauty and elegance to the boys, and to the world. All the girls dress up. Every brain calls up its own image of what to wear when coming out. April Palmieri looks like Alice in Wonderland. Her long dress, decorated all over with flowers and ribbons, is overflowing with grace and romance. Naomi Regelson looks like Marlene Dietrich. More serious and tough, like the cabaret singer in "The Blue Angel."

Ann is wearing her favorite ensemble, strictly Jackie Kennedy: A tight-fitting, peach-colored jacket and short skirt, with a single-strand pearl necklace. High-heel shoes, with hair pinned back severely, crowned by a matching pill-box hat.

The '60s, the pre-hippie '60s, that is, were the source of Ann's sense of style and manner. She said she used to cut out pictures from magazines of the period, and she brought that element, that dignity and severity epitomized by Jackie Kennedy, to the club. But when it got there it was not quite the same.

Her mom is coming to New York next week for a visit. Too bad she isn't here tonight to see Ann's new life in the new world we have constructed together. She might stop worrying that her daughter is so far from her home in West Virginia. There's even a church above the club. Maybe not a splendiferous one, but a church nonetheless.

The boys haven't disappointed us either. They're wearing bright white shorts, and some even have smoking jackets. They know that they are with girls of class.

Confetti, ribbons and balloons fall from the ceiling, as Stanley dances first with April, then with Naomi, and our Master Of Ceremonies Kristian Hoffman croons Elvis's "Love Me Tender."

Can there be anything better than being with friends?

* * *

I am walking slowly to the club. Ann is on duty. I've tried many people out in the past, and usually I end up having to supervise them minutely or even doing the job for them while they watch like slow-motion statues.

But not Ann. If I become dependent upon anyone it will be her. Where did she get that sense of being able to handle any situation? Maybe she was born with it. Maybe her mother carried her a long time in her womb and she developed there to a full and complete state.

She has a lot of respect for everybody, and they respond to this. She is creating her life as an art form like Haring is drawing his pictures.

So I have peace of mind. Until I walk into the club. What greets me there is an unimaginable picture of mayhem. Leonard Abrams, the publisher of the East Village Eye, whom I know as a sensitive kid, runs up to me with a gleam in his eye yelling, "Stanley! Ann is covered with blood!" I rush past him and follow Ann to the locker room. The blood is dripping from her face, down her neck, all over her hands. Upstairs the crowd is yelling like a gang of hooligans.

My heart stops beating for a second and then she is waving her hands and shouting, "I won, I won!"

Back upstairs we see Min, barely five feet tall but a tough contender, being dragged from the wrestling mat screaming, "I'm not finished! I'll get you! you bitch! I'll show you my greatness!" to her friend Stacy Elkin. But the guys muscle her out of the way. That's life. One minute you're up, next you're down.

Around the ring are all the newspaper people: Short Newz, Gore Magazine, Bikini Girl, Punk, and of course, the East Village Eye. Meanwhile the next pair of contestants are sipping grenadine syrup from the bar and holding it in their mouths, in preparation for their bout.

I had forgotten it was Lady Wrestling Night.

* * *

A record sits on my desk with the faces of seven girls floating against a plain white background. April, Jean, Judy, Kim, Min, Stacy, Wendy, all of them from Club 57. Pulsallama has just returned from England after touring with The Clash. I don't know how they managed to arrange that. But Club 57 girls can do a lot.

It was another of Ann's experiments, though she did not stay in the band. This polyrhythmic group sprouted from the Ladies' Auxiliary, and at first with 13 women, "fighting over a cowbell," as the Bush Tetras' guitarist Cynthia Sley once put it, it was another of 57's living parodies.

I have worked with a lot of bands—girl bands, boy bands, all kinds of bands, but this was the craziest of all. This was the art of foolishness, the art of ignorance of music, done very artfully. You have to imagine these wild, insouciant girls, each dressed and made up completely differently, banging on all manner of percussion instruments, sometimes yelling and screaming. A tremendous cacophony. Something like, Listen to us or die. But funny. Maybe it was this light-heartedness that disturbed the other art, punk and art-punk bands. Maybe they were being made fun of!

Drums, tambourines, cowbells and guitars were the main weapons of this satiric carnival. Ann played guitar and sang songs with titles like "Oui-Oui" (a Canadian in Paris)" and "Pulsallama on the Rag." But something else started happening. The girls liked making this racket, and as soon as the band started, real music began to flower inside the noise.

Their first night at club 57 in October of 1981 was indeed a carnival. Nearly everyone in the room had been friends for a couple of years or more. That night was tinged with a slight feeling of loss; you could tell the girls were looking outward with their new project.

"I tell you, boys," said Drew after the gig, "the girls have already ripened. They've become American Amazons."

"So," rejoined Stacey, "You're already jealous of our success?"

"We are, we are. I think that now we're no longer good enough for you. I think, Kenny, that they'll leave us now."

"I did my best to satisfy them," Kenny answered. "But if they leave us we won't cry. We'll find new ones."

John Sex added, "I told you, guys. They've reached their puberty. This is no joke. And we didn't even give them that book to read, 'What Every Girl Should Know About Sex.'"

"That's all you think about!" retorted Ann. What about intellect? And don't masturbate too much because you're losing it."

"But I'll follow you wherever you go," promised John. "You're all my sweetest girls."

Pulsallama started playing all the clubs. And John followed them, taking all the other boys with him.

* * *

Reading Ann's mind:

Here I am in New York with my new friends, but somehow still lonely. And my poor heart is thirsty for some special support.

The boys ... I wonder why Nature created them ...

First it was Peter. His smile was wide and so were his arms. He liked the movies and he knew this neighborhood. It was pretty good to fool around with him. Oh, Peter! He didn't understand that I couldn't spend a lot of time alone with him. He didn't want to hang around the club just to see me. And he likes to cruise around New York with his friends.

Did he have another girl? I wonder. I wish he could have been more like Kristian {Hoffman}, who is much more into art, and more mature. But Kristian had a girlfriend.

I'm too busy. That's why we fought so much. And then he split ...

Some boys are so young emotionally—even if they are only two years older than me they think I'm old. But, being platonic friends, we developed a real addiction to each other. Pure love. Now I understand how Stanley feels.

Then there was Eric. He is very interested in the music and performances we have at the club, like me. He is very delicate, gentle and shy. He won't yell at me. He helps me at the club. Besides, he is a tall, good-looking boy. I like his narrow hips in those black leather pants. And his eyes, too.

I don't know what's going on with me. And I don't know what kind of boyfriend I should have. Maybe I do know, but I haven't met him yet. With Eric, we are more friends than lovers. I get so tired from working at the club that I don't have the energy to get excited about much else. I might as well work in a coal mine. It might be easier.

Stanley had a very good idea with Irving Plaza. He spent a lot of time and money to open the place for rock'n'roll. He wanted to create a good club in New York, and with his imagination and dedication he will have it. He already got a contract to supply the best bands from Europe and the best events in New York. And what happened? Those greedy idiots locked us out. Now Stanley has to suffer, and the club too …

I've been here two years now. How long will I be scrubbing the floor, talking to all the kids in New York who want to have an evening at the club? This is the worst club I've ever seen. Tiny, low ceiling, no windows, lousy air conditioning, broken chairs. I have to smile constantly at the cops who answer the neighbors' complaints about noise and crowds on the sidewalk. Then I have to fight just to get a few dollars' rent for the church.

Yesterday we had a beer delivery, and where was Stanley? The last I saw of him was when that lady from the church called him away with a funny smile. What were they doing in the upper hall? Chasing the devil to Hell like in the Decameron? He came back looking tired and droopy-eyed. I'm sure they had some kind of adventure up there.

And what about my career? I wonder if I have any wrinkles yet. Steve Mass keeps coming around offering me deals to defect to the Mudd Club. He's completely obsessed about Club 57. He even threw his own birthday party here instead of his own club. Stanley feels change is coming, but he doesn't say anything. He even gave Steve a big hug.

Now I'm doing my own shows, here and at other places. It's too much, it's killing me. But look at Stanley. He has to work another job to keep this place alive. But what does he think, that I'm a horse? Can't he see I need help? Why isn't he a millionaire?

Two years at Club 57. And what do I have to show for it? The school of life, I guess. But I want to go to Broadway, to Hollywood. Will I ever get there, staying in this broken-down club?

The club isn't these walls, it's the people who come here. And I love them. But …

…We loved her too. Ann resigned as manager of Club 57 in 1981, and began a series of shows around town, and then eventually all over the country, with her distinct and very ironic brand of performance. She was replaced by her assistant Andy Rees, and then by Ira Abramowitz, both of whom brought great energies to the club until their personal lives got in the way, as we will see. But the Club 57 crowd always followed Ann wherever she performed, as if she was another Judy Garland. And so did I.

She became a Goddess of Downtown New York culture, spreading the Club 57 mentality all over the world. Look around—you can see it today.

* * *

Ann had always wanted to perform. As a teenager in Charleston, NC, she studied acting, music and dance, and played Helen Keller in a production of "The Miracle Worker." She lived in London before moving to New York, where she acted in a rewritten production of Moliere's "Les Precieuses Ridicules."

Ann brought her spirit, wit and the punk cynicism of post-Vietnam American youth to Club 57, where it blossomed into a thousand different projects. After she left Club 57, she continued to work with Keith Haring and Kenny Scharf on their exhibitions, while performing her many personas around town, which included a heavy metal rocker in her band Bongwater.

She began acting in films, first in a minor part as a victim of David Bowie's vampire in "The Hunger," then in a leading role with John Malkovich in Susan Seidelman's "Making Mr. Right." Ann followed up that success in "A Night in the Life of Jimmy Reardon," appearing with River Phoenix. She has done two solo video features, "Made For TV" and "Vandemonium," that appeared on PBS and HBO. And she has played supporting roles on ABC's TV sitcom, "Anything But Love." My favorite piece of all time was "You Could Be Home Now," a performance she gave at Lincoln Center.

I visited Ann in Hollywood. I loved Palm Boulevard in Santa Monica. That steep, high bank reminded me of the shores of Ireland. I walked the beach, picking up shells and stones for my collection. My mother and my wife Grace watched the sandpipers run with lightning steps away from the surf, then run back again. I can spend hours watching them, and the disappearing sun, changing the water into flames.

We met at a Thai restaurant with some of Ann's new friends. She was still struggling at the time. "Everybody has a soul full of dreams," I told her, "usually not accomplished. They are our engine of activity. You dream about fame, and you are going after it."

"You know, Stanley, there are millions of actors and actresses in America—many of them very talented too. How will I ever stand out against that competition?"

"Ann, you are very stubborn and brave, like a fisherman on the open sea, like Hemingway's "The Old Man and the Sea." But you are young and strong, and you will overcome the sharks."

We went to the Avenue of the Stars for ice cream, where I gave her a present, a painting on fabric of her idol Jim Morrison. We had three different kinds of ice cream with sprinkles and strawberries, and I licked my fingers and asked for seconds like a kid, and felt jealous of her friends, knowing I would no longer see her delicate hands and share her secrets, creations and dreams.

Some time before I arrived in Hollywood, Ann sent me a card. It read, "Thank you, Stanley, for telling me to search for God mostly in people's hearts. You were right."

So the Alabaster Girl went to Hollywood searching for happiness. Well, I guess if she can find it there, she can find it anywhere.

Chapter Eight

Father's Day

June 15, 1980. I've passed my 30th birthday some time ago. Let me see the mirror. Looks like not many wrinkles yet. Some circles under my eyes. Cheeks pretty smooth. Even losing some hair in front doesn't take my young look and feeling away. Still a cute, boyish-looking creature. How long will that be true when I miss sleeping several nights in a row because of work?

In Poland I had several girlfriends, but I have lost them and my best friends forever by moving to New York. Here the boys and girls make me feel comfortable, lending me their spirit and enthusiasm. It has extended my youth. I am even afraid of older people. They have lost the use of those two words. Tonight I should probably look more official and serious. Ann and Susan were very stubborn: they insisted on making a party for me. On Father's Day I was mad. I thought they were treating me as a friend, but now I know there is some screen between us. Or maybe it's just my way of thinking. They explained to me that they want only to give me special respect because I am the father and founder of the club. Then why do they never curse me, push me or joke at my expense? I am sure they're not afraid of me. They feel so free here.

So I decide to put on a shirt and tie—let's make a double Italian knot—then suit and polished shoes. I really don't know. I don't feel good in it anymore. But my Mom says, "It's OK, Stan. You look a little like a mannequin from a Saks department store window. But today it's all right. Sometimes it's good to change."

Now I am feeling nostalgic. I sift through my paperboard box of memorabilia: notebooks, fragments of newspapers, leaflets, club programs, bills, fines, letters fall out. There are still a few that have not disappeared over the many years, that my wife hasn't managed to throw away yet. In the bottom of the box playing dead are things that can talk. Here are a few gifts from the club crew that I received on Fathers Day. An old fountain pen from Jeffrey Geiger. "It's a souvenir from my Dad," he says, "And it works. You just fill the inkwell, then pull the spring on the side." I remember it from my childhood—pens like that and notebooks full of blots.

Then there is the hand-painted picture of two horses painted by Susan's uncle. Horses dancing on a lawn near a forest. What a wonderful feeling to look at that picture! I immediately see myself there, at one with nature, breathing fresh air, the greenness of the grass giving my eyes so much relaxation. If they weren't two Pegasuses, maybe it's only because Uncle forgot to paint wings on them.

Lets see what Kenny has for me: Two plastic dinosaurs. This is his world of fantasy, and in it he is giving me part of himself. Very proud, he was, looking at me and saying, "But don't let eat them. Let them grow. They're so small, just kids."

Then Keith grabs the left side of my jacket and pins on a handpainted button reading: "Stanley's Club 57."

After a while I shift my gaze from the paperboard box to one on the shelf, made of plastic. Inside is a dried red rose. I won't lie to you. This is from a boy, not a girl. From Andy Rees. A dried past. And it still looks good after more than 15 years. Andy was a very active member and Ann's right hand. When Ann left I took him on as the club manager. I never got a rose from anyone else in my life. Especially not a boy. But my wife looked at that rose very suspiciously. Maybe she is jealous. I wonder how long the rose will remain here.

I turn my eyes again to the box. On the very bottom are two postcards. One is from John Sex. What do you expect from him? A couple on the beach in embracing in love. As he gave it his eyes twinkled.

The other card is from Tom Scully—a picture of Babe Ruth, and the message, "Stanley, you'll go down in history as one of our truly great Americans." Some exaggeration. I prefer money to fame. It can keep me alive.

And I went down, but not in history. And there's one more under the two cards: The book from Ann. Black art photography. Sand creatures from Florida beaches. There are not many other relics left.

It was really a family evening. There weren't many strangers around, just the girls and boys who were closest to me. Their eyes shone with honesty, and I felt their great hearts. Andy, with his typical sense of the absurd, sang sentimental songs to me for the enjoyment of all.

John hid the few good chairs we had, the put the most broken ones in front. Then he put one close to Drew and invited him to sit on it: "Why are you standing like a candle? You must be tired after the orgy at Monster Night."

So Drew tried to sit and of course the chair collapsed. He sprang to his feet and ran after John. When he caught him they both ended up on the floor, and John started in with his usual claim of "Help! He's trying to rape me! I'm innocent!"

This forced Ann to step into her role as arbiter of disputes. She got them both chairs and then said to me, "Stanley, as the oldest, I think you can pass judgment on John. "Of course," I cried. "If he can prove he is really sexy as he claims, I will forgive him his tricks with the chair."

"Oh God, I'm saved," exclaimed John. And he loosened the top button on his pants. But that only showed a little of his hips, to prove that, with the absence of underwear, his fashion sense was au courant. This was before Calvin Klein was exploiting the underwear-exposed, jailbird look. But Dany Johnson, the pint-sized DJ who admired John very much, suddenly pulled the front of his jeans down to exhibit his hips more full. The girls approved of this, screaming, "He is, he is!" So the girls judged that he indeed was living up to his name, and John Sex avoided punishment for his misbehavior.

And Drew added, "And he has to get it out of his head that I'm going to be his boyfriend." The girls agreed, stating, "Better stay with girls. It's time."

My mother had been sitting with Susan in the corner but the commotion brought them to the front. "What's happening?" she asked. "Why did John's pants fall down?"

"He got too horny," Drew answered. "His pants got strained and the button took off like a shot!" But my Mom just smiled and said,

"Before it goes too far and I leave, let me show you the album I have of Stanley when he was a teenager and a young man. Would you like to see it?" "Oh yes," said Kenny. How old is Stanley now?" "29.99." I replied.

"That's cheaper than on Orchard Street, but there's probably some tax." "Who's that?" asked Ann.

"That's Stanley," Mom explained. "He was playing Joseph at the Catholic Theater in the production of Zawieyski's "The River of Adversity," which is where the Broadway show 'Joseph and the Amazing Technicolor Dreamcoat' came from.

Here he's in the Army, where he ran the Cabaret Variety Show, when he wasn't learning how to crawl in the mud."

More and more pictures, "After he came out of the Army he worked for a construction company, and then he ran a laundry business with me. It was no way to get rich, but that was impossible in Poland then anyway."

"What beautiful mountains." Ann says.

"He belonged to the Tourist Club," recalled Mom, "under the leadership of the painter Wieslaw Matuszek. Maybe there are too many girls in the pictures with him, but he was a funny boy, always joking and organizing some events, and everybody liked it."

Yes, I remember it well. We hiked all over Poland with rucksacks on our backs, fully equipped to eat and sleep out for days at a time.

We traveled around the Baltic Sea Coast, across the Great Valley to the Tatra Mountains. I felt very close to the country. I will always love those forest paths, lakes, streams, fields, which at springtime are mosaics of green, red and white. In the autumn were golden stands of grain, piled high in haystacks. I remember jumping on the rocks of the Karkonosze Mountains, hiking at Bieszczady and the Tatra mountains, snowcapped well into the summer. In the summer there were sand dunes and beaches on the Baltic Sea, the waves cuddling my feet. But mostly I recall the villages and their hospitable people. Many times I asked them for milk and their delicious country bread, and they never would take anything for it.

You still can find them in Poland. I recently went back for a visit, and hiked with friends across a gorgeous part of Poland called "Kaszuby Switzerland," with a hundred lakes and fairytale hills. And I can't forget that happy mother of six children, Irena Kotlowska of Mirachowo, who gave me two gallons of fresh milk with that specific smell of the cow.

Vagabonding, wandering and hiking, I learned how to eat meals from the same plate with my friends, how to love people around me and how to love nature.

The boys and girls were still looking at my picture book. "And you also have a picture of Fred Astaire here," says Naomi. "Was he your idol?"

"Yes, he was. I always danced. I started learning from my sister Danuta and her friends. She was a teenager and I was just seven years old. I belonged to dance groups in school as well."

"And here, what is that building with such big columns?"

My Mom answers, "That's just a building in Warsaw. We were coming from Auschwitz. Stan took me there. He wanted to see it.

"How did the war touch your family?" asked Keith.

"Many in my family were shot, or they went to labor or concentration camps. How I avoided it was a miracle. I had many Jewish neighbors. One of them sent me a letter from the Warsaw Ghetto. They had no food and were starving to death. So I decided to go there. I took a loaf of bread and some smoked meat, hiding it in the top of the country wagon I hitched a ride in. On the way a German patrol stopped us. They asked if I was smuggling anything. I said no. They found the food and took it away. Maybe because I was young and the German wasn't too old, he didn't shoot me. He just slapped my face. My sister-in-law Zosia wasn't that lucky. She was shot for no reason a few days later.

"Stop, Mother,' I interrupted. "It's too much."

"I just answered the question, didn't I?" she replied. She looked around at us.

"And here," said Jeffrey quickly, "there's an ocean liner with you up at the front."

"That's the boat on which I came to America," I said. "It was some adventure, because of the storm we went through. The waves were 12 yards high—the boat was dancing. I was sick and throwing up, but mentally I felt good. I badly wanted to be in a storm in the ocean after reading Joseph Conrad."

"What about this church?" asks April.

"That's not a church. That's the Town Hall in the middle of the Old City of Gdansk."

I miss the city of my youth, one of the loveliest in Europe. For over a thousand years it has been the main port of Poland. Around the city there are high, forested hills, only now the forest is within the city itself. There I used to go skiing every winter. Skiing nighttime was best, with only the moon and stars to see by.

Now a great noise is coming from the front of the club. It's Denise, pushing her young brother Harley, who is kicking all the garbage cans as he walks. The kid is carrying a guitar, trying to play a song, his eyes shining with excitement.

Then Denise suddenly stops and cries out, "Oh no, Stan. What did you do to yourself?" She spits on the floor. "It's such a great day for you and you dress up like some jerky yuppie. Can't you wear normal clothes? Aren't you ashamed in front of the younger generation?"

I look at their "normal clothing": Army boots, ripped black jeans and leather jackets full of chains, more chains around her neck. And a fresh tattoo on the arm of proud Harley.

"I'm in business. Sometimes I have to blend with the hypocritical society which cares more about their strange uniform than expressing their inner beauty." "At least you have your broken tooth—if not, I wouldn't recognize you." And she punched my chest. I almost fell over.

Behind her are the rest of the Stimulators. And the Invaders, the Misfits, the New York Niggers, the Marbles, the Nails, Mars, the Public Problems, the Fleshtones and the Zantees. And Nervous Rex. And more. Then the Foolish Virgins with Steve McEvoy, who starts to play the song he played two years ago in "Cowboy Mouth." It's no longer possible to control the noise, or the joy. And nobody needs to smoke pot to be high.

Chapter Nine

Helen's Pierogis and the Party at Princess Pamela's

Things were going pretty well. It seems I could do a lot with these nice people as we work towards complete success.

So I started thinking of how to get them together, how to get closer to their hearts. They are lonely, lost in New York like myself. And so we are finding ourselves.

With that in mind I organized a trip to West Point by boat. That way we would be forced to spend four hours together each way on the Day Line cruiser. We'd have time to speak out, to chart the courses of each other's hearts, and grow closer to each other and to nature.

So, one Sunday in May of 1979 we met at the 43rd Street pier on the Hudson River. Included in the group were Susan Hannaford, John Sex, Tom Scully, Irving Plaza bartender Jeffrey Geiger, the band booker Cathy Gallagher, and John Richard, the house manager of Irving Plaza at the time. Even my mom, Helen Lembryck, came along. It was too bad that Ann Magnuson couldn't come—she was too busy with the new program at the little Club 57 on St. Mark's Place.

The ship offered a buffet, but we decided it would be much better to bring our own food. What could be better than eating sandwiches provided by Susan, Cathy's salad and a surprise dish made by my Mom? There was also cheesecake, fruit, vegetables, boiled eggs, and a whole cooler full of soda and juice that Tom and John brought.

In the morning, a cool, light breeze from the hills of New Jersey caused us to take shelter behind the wall of the boat's superstructure. Between the wind and our talking, our throats got pretty dry, and we made a big dent in the supply of juice and soda.

Even thought the boat had barely passed under the Washington Bridge, we suddenly got hungry as well, though probably due as much to our sociable mood than any physical need. We also began to shake off the sleepy, melancholy mood that came of our being unaccustomed to waking so early, and feasted our eyes on the fresh green hills of New Jersey, as we steamed up the Hudson toward Bear Mountain and West Point. The temperature was rising as we admired the fruit tree blossoms along the West Side Highway, and we moved to the upper level and stretched out on the deck chairs, and watched the shapes of the clouds.

The conversation eventually started drift from club talk to more relaxing topics. "Why is it called the Hudson River?" asked my mother.

"Henry Hudson was the famed discoverer and traveler. He was looking, like the others, for a passageway to India," I explained. "He thought this was it. When he found out it wasn't, he tried farther north and ended up discovering Hudson's Bay in Canada."

"And what then? did he find the way to India?"

"He couldn't do it."

"Why? Did someone else get there first?"

"No, there was a mutiny on his ship. The crew left him and his young son on a small boat, and from that time on they were lost without a trace."

"So that's how it is," said Tom. "Crazy, brave people blaze a path for humanity to follow, but perish for their efforts."

The hours passed, and we became restless. Finally, with only 30 minutes left before we reached West Point, Mom pulled out her surprise dish. It was in a jar, so large that she could hardly get it out of her bag, and still wrapped in a towel to keep its contents warm.

A wonderful smell is seeping out of the jar, and everyone is trying to guess what's inside.

"Kielbasy," says Susan.

"Golombki (stuffed cabbage)," I say.

"Whatever it is it must by Polish," says Cathy. She has been watching John, who she knows better than anybody else and, seeing the sparks in his eyes, she knows he must be remembering some kind of food his grandmother made for him a long time ago, when he was a little boy.

"It's pierogis!" yells John, handing the jar to Cathy.

Cathy opens the jar and everyone can now smell the meat, onions and gravy inside. By the time the pier of West Point was in view, we were licking our fingers. John almost ate the plates. He would have licked the jar too, I believe, if he could have fit his head inside, but when he finished his portion, he got that angelic look on his face, and he was ready to love the whole world.

Then we left the boat to explore the historic buildings and grounds of West Point. We took a few pictures in front of the statues of General Washington and General Tadeusz Kosciuszko, the Polish patriot who was the founder and builder of the West Point Military Academy. The most interesting place was the Military Museum. There we relived the history of the United States Army, which in the Museum was shown intertwined with that of the Allied countries, especially in the case of World War II. It was a good illustration of the power of human solidarity, and cooperation against some devil's ideology.

The few hours we spent at West Point went quickly, and soon it was time to take the boat back to our lovely city, New York, to seek refuge in its walls.

As Jeffrey opened a bottle of brandy, Mom took the opportunity to ask John, "Why haven't you gotten married yet?"

"A while ago my girlfriend pushed me to get married," John explained. "So I went to her father and I told him I wanted to marry her. But he kicked me out and I was saved."

Probably the brandy went to his head because he continued, "Anyway, I was glad. Her father was a heavy drinker. I found that out when I saw him drunk, yelling that he wasn't afraid of his wife.

"But that's not all. Once we went to the theater together and he left after the first act. Later he explained that the program said the second part would take place two years later.

"And last month I saved a good friend of mine. He wanted to borrow two thousand dollars for his wedding, but I refused to lend it to him."

"You have a lot of experience," said Mom. "You know many stories."

"I can tell you more," answered John, "if you tell me the secret of your pierogi recipe. I've never had anything like them in any of the Polish restaurants in New York."

"That recipe was given to me by my mother, Mary, so my whole life I've made them only this way.

"The secret is that you have to mix two kinds of meat together with fresh cabbage and sauerkraut. You also add the dry Boletus mushrooms called "Borowiki" in Polish, plus onions, and a good amount of pepper. Then you wrap them in dough and boil them.

"The onions {for the garnish} are also prepared a special way. You put a very small amount of oil in a pot and fry them until they are brown. Before you put them on top of the pierogis you can add a little butter to them. And then you eat them."

"Are you going to do it again?" asks Susan.

"Yes, I'm sure."

"Then let's not tell John next time. He'll eat everything."

By the time we got home, we were so tired from our adventure that we didn't go to the club until the following evening.

We loved being together for all kinds of private events, and many times I would take a bunch of people out for dinner. The next time this happened, Ann Magnuson and Chris Gremski were part of the group. We went to a Japanese restaurant in Greenwich Village.

At the time there weren't that many Japanese restaurants in New York. We liked it because we could sit on the floor eating oriental plates full of very fresh sushi. The décor lifted us to a different part of the world without leaving the city.

We would eat in a Greek restaurant on 15th Street or an Indian restaurant on 6th Street, or a Jewish place called the Second Avenue Deli, near 10th Street. The Ukrainian restaurant, the Kiev, was another popular spot, especially with Ann. Then, when I opened my restaurant on First Avenue, we ate under the paintings of Kenny Scharf and Keith Haring, and posters made by John Sex.

But pizza was always the staple food of Club 57, eaten at the corner or brought to the club for consumption.

Another time, Keith took me, John and his buddy Shawn McQuate to the Metropolitan Museum of Art. We spent just a few hours on the ground floor, looking at the modern art collection, which included Picasso, Matisse and Chagall. But they weren't just looking at the pictures. The paintings seared them with passion. Their eyes devoured every movement of the painters' brushes, as they searched for the sense and soul of each picture.

We had agreed it was to be Keith's day, so we didn't argue when he kept us there, refusing to explore any further in the museum. After we left we had a picnic at Cleopatra's Needle, the obelisk in Central Park not far from the Museum. We stayed there until dark, musing about the art of Egypt, spellbound by that obelisk, which told us that there was more to be gained from reading its hieroglyphics in the bonds of imagination and human fellowship than from nearly any book.

Perhaps the most interesting thing that happened on our restaurant forays was the time we went to Princess Pamela's on 10th Street and First Avenue, located on the second floor of a mysterious two-story building whose windows were always covered by curtains, while the door was always closed.

This secretive house always fascinated me, and I decided to find out what was happening on the other side of the sign that only announced the name of someone inside. One day I pressed the bottom bell in the entranceway. A window opened on the second floor and a smiling face asked me, "May I help you, dear?"

I realized that if I needed help for any reason, I needed it from her.

"I am looking for Princess Pamela."

"She is home."

"May I come inside?"

"Yes you may."

When I reached the second floor I was met by a very distinguished-looking African American woman, who welcomed me and said, "This is a private party house. If you wish, you can make a reservation for any evening you want."

I was very curious and a little excited about this place, and I decided right then to have a party there.

Two days later I arrived with eight Club 57 members. Princess Pamela and her assistant served us very good chicken, salad and boiled vegetables. We liked the place because the dinner was very inexpensive, and we were touched by the charm of the hostess, but we were really impressed by the décor. The room had a real countrified, family feeling to it, and we felt like we were guests in someone's house, maybe in California.

One of the guests, Shawn McQuate, became so hooked on the charm of the Princess's "palace" that he promptly booked it for his upcoming birthday party, inviting 20 friends from the club. The little money he had had become "big bucks" in his imagination, and the price of the party, according to him, would be so low as to be almost nothing at all.

The Princess was very excited too, knowing that famous people from New York's "art society" would also be there. At least that's what her door assistant told me.

I went upstairs with Susan, Ann and Tom. In the first room a jazz group called the Street Band welcomed us with lovely syncopated tunes. At the next doorway was Shawn himself, with a smile that stretched ear to ear. The room was so crowded that it was difficult to move. Once we sat down at our table, we knew we had to remain seated. John Sex was helping his friend Shawn, and regaling us with stories about him.

"You know," he said, "that Shawn is a prince from North Carolina. That's why he wanted to have a party in this 'palace.' For sure he's King tonight."

"Oh, yeah!" everybody yelled. We all loved Shawn for the charm, friendliness and sense of fantasy that he gave to all the club activities.

"Viva Prince Shawn!"

John opened a bottle of champagne and poured it all around. I think only he, with his narrow hips, could have maneuvered between all the chairs and bodies. The remainder of the champagne he poured first over Shawn's head, then his. Then he grabbed Shawn and, with the help of Kenny Scharf and Min Sanchez, they flung Shawn up in the air. Then came the brandy, which made the kids crazy. They piled all the chairs into a pyramid, which left us room to walk around and later to rip Shawn's shirt off in a cuddling hysteria.

Some strange smell was coming from among the musicians. I secretly asked Princess Pamela, "Are we allowed to smoke grass here? Is it a private club?"

"By the law, you're not supposed to, Mr. Stanley," answered the Princess.

I became angry at that. In this aristocratic setting, she hadn't addressed me as "Lord Stanley." But I swallowed my pride.

To pay further homage to our host, a few kids put him on a table and, in a mock orgy, kissed him all over and pinched him Italian style. But then the Princess started ringing her dinner bell, announcing that her delicious chicken was about to be served.

At this point Shawn's shirt was no more, so he just put his white jacket on. It was difficult for everyone to cool down, but we were hungry by now, and from the kitchen a wonderful smell attacked our noses. The ladies had used many kinds of herbs and spices. That's the East Village style of American meal: spices, herbs and a Princess to prepare it.

The Princess, who had worked very hard up to this point, left us briefly. She returned with a new costume, a stunning long gown and sparkling jewelry. Suddenly I realized that this lady, possessed of so much gentleness, had more nobility than one could hope to find among any of the "registered" aristocracy.

I never returned to her palace. But she and that place remain in an exalted spot in my memory.

Shawn felt like an angel in heaven, and maybe even like a priest at a religious lesson, because he asked everybody, "Who wants to go to Heaven?"

We thought about the Heaven we had right there, with Shawn, the Princess and those nice people in the "Street Band."

Everybody raised their hands and yelled, "We do!"

Everyone, that is, except Ann, who was sitting with Princess Pamela. She didn't say a word. "Don't you want to go to Heaven?" the Princess asked her.

"No," she answered. "I have to go to the club, and see what's going on." Then she hugged Princess Pamela and Shawn and left the party.

Then the bill came. It was over $400. Shawn realized of a sudden that Heaven cost more than he thought. Susan grabbed the bill and told me, "Stanley, look at this crazy, happy guy. He doesn't have enough to pay for the party!"

Fortunately I had some extra cash with me, and I paid the rest of it. It just goes to show you these days not every aristocrat has money.

Chapter Ten

My Colorful Dream

(introduction to The Painters)

My newest friend is Nicole Peterson, who is five years old and likes to dance with me. She has black eyes like two coals and such a live temperament that she can transport the most phlegmatic among us.

Yesterday I gave her a green plastic bird-whistle that trills like a warbler when you put a little water in it. Now she informs me with great sorrow that she has lost it.

"Nicole," I said, "You see, you had a bird and you lost the bird. But don't worry, you will have another one or maybe a better toy. Everything that we have is only for a certain time. This is not easy to understand, but you have to learn it and not be constantly sad."

Nicole looked at me and said, "Good, but this time buy me a pink bird," and filled with anticipation of the new bird, stopped being sad. Nicole will learn that everything is passing and new things are created. She will experience meetings and partings, like birth and death, like destroying and creating. Tomorrow maybe she won't have it, and she will love what she has, like passing dreams. Colorful dreams. The pictures of her life. The picture of human life, which people have painted from thousands of years ago in grottoes in France, or yesterday in the studios of the Impressionists.

But something from these living pictures stays with us forever, sometimes engraved in deep furrows and wrinkles in our foreheads and crows' feet near our eyes. They create the living picture of our personalities—the picture of our lives engraved on our faces and our souls in a kind of life-made impressionism. We live now in an era in which we constantly search for new forms of expression. We look for new ways to express ourselves in art.

Chief among these is pop, which exposes the psyche of the human being to the common person after it has been buried by modern existence. Pop reaches out to modern humanity, touching the hearts and minds of the millions.

Though pop art as a movement began decades ago, its aftershock in the '70s and '80s amplified it to new heights, to the point that it is now found in every corner of the world.

One place in which it sprang forth with vast energy was in the basement in New York City that became Club 57. The colorful picture it made was my living dream, my dreaming reality.

Chapter Eleven

The Painters

The trinity of painters who emerged from Club 57 to gain fame for their extraordinary achievements consisted of Jean-Michel Basquiat, Keith Haring and Kenny Scharf. Keith came from Pennsylvania, Kenny from California and Jean-Michel from Brooklyn. They had their first exhibitions at the club, but more than that, as they began their careers they used it as their headquarters and second home, spending nearly every day there meeting with friends and sharing their personal and artistic lives with the 100 or so members. It became a livingroom for a very large family.

I will not attempt to explicate the works of these three: a number of books have been written about them that will do the job better. I wish rather to tell of some things they did and we did together that may give an idea of the life they held within them.

All my life I have been fascinated by the lives of artists, many of whom met with tragedy, such as Goya, El Greco, Michelangelo, Modigliani, Lautrec and Van Gogh. Afraid of hunger, I have never been able to sacrifice bread for art. For this reason I admire all the more the persistence of vision that drove these artists to create, whether hungry, sick or haunted by their personal demons, without regard for their own well-being. Of the three artists to emerge brilliantly from Club 57, two paid the ultimate price for the lives they led.

The first exhibition of the three was an evening full of joy and hope. It was our own exhibition; we weren't waiting around for the public to arrive. We were just happy to see our own members' works on the walls, displaying drastically different techniques. Keith drew his pictures in chalk or Magic Marker. His lines were perfect, mature and precise, a contrast of white on black or vice-versa. Each image was full of a deep sense, content and spirit. There was nobody in the room whom his art didn't touch. We didn't understand his greatness, but we already felt it. The lines were so gently and easily put down on paper and canvas, reminding me of Cocteau or Picasso. The noble lines communicated his heart and mind in a way a child could understand, before his eyes are closed by the deceit we are told is maturity.

Keith's paintings made us realize how much our soul is the soul of a child, with the thirst for goodness and the demand for the world to be better. For this Keith used as his symbol the "Radiant Baby," the image of an infant surrounded by rays of light, because this was in fact his nature. In this way he reminds me of Chopin, whose perfect, unaccompanied tones I compare with the spare perfection of Keith's lines. I like to play Chopin recordings when I look at Keith's art. They both gave so much from their natures, and their complicated human souls.

Later Keith started to use color to make his pictures more alive, but almost always it was the drawing that gave his images strength. But, like Chopin, Haring's paintings gave a thousand colors to our imagination, and this is their greatest triumph.

The art of Haring is also brave. He wasn't afraid to open his soul, his dreams, his personality. His life is spoken through his pictures. It addresses his feelings of friendship, his yearning for love. He was brave like his friend Madonna. Both of them grew up in hypocritical times, when shame surrounds issues of sex and religion, marking contemporary artists both dead and alive. Their bravery I cannot achieve, and for this I envy them.

At the opening of this first exhibition I gazed at Keith's "Dancing Boys," a large painting on paper, and it reminded me very much of "The Dancing," a Matisse that exists in two versions, one of which hangs in the museum in St. Petersburg, the other in the Museum Of Modern Art in New York.

"What do you think about it?" Keith asked after suddenly appearing behind me. His eyes were exalted with a profusion of light; my reaction was important to him.

"I like it very much," I told him. "The boys are dancing freely like

Fred Astaire." I do love dance deep in my heart. I liked the picture; I wanted the picture, but, like Haring himself, I was shy. Mostly I bought the drawings of caricaturist Daniel Ethan Abraham, but this was different. I could have asked him for the picture using my standing as the club's director, but I could not bring myself to. But Keith, meanwhile, wanted to give it to me as much as I wanted it. He volunteered, "It will be yours when the exhibition is finished." And, smiling, he added, "Stan, you're always so good to everybody here. You got us together, and I really found a home here. You are a man with a wide-open mind. We all respect that." So after the show I took the picture and put it in my new Polish restaurant on First Avenue, to join a poster of John Sex and a Technicolor fantasy painting by Kenny Scharf.

Keith was the shyest boy of any of them. But his voice rang loud in the expression of the things he cared about: injustice, life, fate, death, human sexuality, homosexual and otherwise, and love.

Nevertheless his art is very joyous. Always in them you can see the humanism, and the wish to create a better world.

Keith Haring, Kenny Scharf, John Sex and Drew Straub were the closest of friends at that time, the years 1979 and 1980. They worked together to decorate the club for many of our events. They were the most creative and active members during that time, working with Ann Magnuson, whom I hired as manager.

It was Keith who organized the "Sex In Art" show in 1979, showcasing his and other club artists' views of one of their favorite subjects. This show was very explicit, showing many details and nuances of nature's glorious gift of regeneration and pleasure. We all agreed that New York needed more of this kind of art, rather than the poor substitutes found on 42nd Street. We were pleased that we could help people learn to enjoy sex without feelings of shame and fear, homophobia, and denial of sexual urges. How ironic to see that the people most upset about sexuality are the ones going to the porno stores!

Soon after it opened the Bishop of the church walked in and pulled me aside. Coming in behind him were some Sanitation Department workers, who started looking at the show. "Look, Stan," said the Bishop. "People have been calling me and the people who work in the building, saying that this is not really a cultural club, that you're running some kind of pornography show here. They're trying to use it to discredit me. What kind of art is this? New Wave? Look at that huge penis on the bar. Is that art?"

I answered him, "I'm sure you studied art at the Seminary. I did, and I know that the phallus was a part of worship in many ancient cultures. Do you remember the statue of the phallus on the Greek island of Delos, or its many representations in Laotian and Indian temples, as symbols of fertility and delight? And how about the many sexual scenes on the temples at Khajurano?" Too bad I didn't know then about the wonderful Sister Wendy, the nun who is also an art critic, and described in such a natural way the acts of the human body, stating that it is all a beautiful part of heaven's creation.

The Bishop didn't say anything, perhaps stymied by my answer, as well as the eyes of Ann, standing next to the huge cock. But the sanitation workers, who sometimes dropped by to say hello to Ann and get a cold drink, had something to say. They looked at the free expression of sexuality around them and said to the Bishop, "This isn't porno, even if it looks primitive. This is art, and we like it!"

The Bishop, who must have been relieved to hear this support from among the working people, replied, "Yes, Michelangelo had the same problem when he painted the Sistine Chapel." And he left us alone. So you see, even a bishop can learn about art.

Several months later Keith moved on to become a member of the "famous artists" club. But he kept his friendships alive, and often returned to the club to take part in our activities.

The year was 1985 and I had just gotten married, and Ann Magnuson had a birthday party in the newly-opened bar Beulah-Land, run by Susan Hannaford-Rose, previously known for operating the Monster Movie Club with Tom Scully. My wife Grace wore the richly decorated wedding dress she had brought from her home in Shanghai. Keith came together with Kenny to congratulate us. They were already famous by that time. Keith gave me a hug and said, "Stan, it was the most beautiful time in my life. I was poor but happy. You see how life is. Why couldn't we be together forever? I wish we had never split. It will never happen again so good and colorful. It can't. You see how life is." The most splendid picture painted in our lives, gone. Maybe it is forever in the museums of our hearts.

I pulled his ear and said, "You were my kid and you always will be." Then he laughed and said, "You're lucky, you can have a relationship with girls. You know what I mean. I'm always looking for a happy personal life, and it's not so easy. Good luck for you and your wife, and for your wonderful mom."

I saw Keith again at the memorial service for our friend and painter Jean-Michel Basquiat at the church of St. Peter on 53rd Street in 1988. Keith came in a light overcoat. He was serious but very controlled. His face had become more oval, and it seemed more noble than any time before. Keith had contracted AIDS some time before, and it had begun to act upon him. His sickness gave his face a special expression of infinity, as if it tried to say, I will live forever.

"So you see, Stan, we see each other again. The world is so small. Looks like our life runs so quickly and dramatically. Too fast for many. And there is so much to do. You see, we loved Jean-Michel very much. He was our kid, your kid too. He will know what we feel about him and he will be with us forever, won't he?"

I said to him, "Everything that he achieved was his joy of friendship with you and the other New York kids. The world didn't give him too much. The richness of his deep, enthusiastic soul was so great, and he always wanted to tell everybody that he missed the paradise that was not on this earth."

Keith looked at me again like he did like the time he did his first installation at Club 57. I touched his left cheek. We gave each other a melancholy smile. He gave my mom a hug. The last hug. Keith's membership number was 35. And he died February 16th, 1990 at the age of 31. New York cried for him. The Radiant Baby showed on the Times Square electronic billboard for a month.

Keith Haring had a strong connection with Kenny Scharf through the bonds of friendship. Kenny painted happier, funnier pictures, using a lot of color and fantasy from his younger years of life, drawing from animated television cartoons. He had a fascination with toys and dinosaurs as well. He uses all kinds of materials in his compositions. It could be something he found on the street, or in some basement or attic. His pictures were cascades of color and fantasy, unlocked from his childhood. He was very handsome, and more aggressive personally than Keith, unceremonious in speech, and not afraid to fight for his point of view.

Kenny's first presentation at the club was a parody of a go-go performance, in which he, John Sex and Sean McQuate frolicked, made faces and stripped (though only to their bathing suits), while the girls of the club yelled and screamed with laughter. Everybody fell in love with these three handsome boys, and the flavor of sex that emanated from them united everyone in the room in a kind of collective ecstasy. It may be from that performance that Keith got his idea for his "Dancing Boys" painting. I can't say for sure. But I am sure that the colors and vitality of Kenny's paintings came from the active way in which he gave himself to his art.

I also saw in him a boy who liked to play in the realm of pre-adult life to escape from the envy, hypocrisy and deceit of this world. And when I look at a Scharf painting I receive so much energy that I want to dance, sing, yell and speak crazy and wise things together with the characters he paints. And I don't need anyone around me: I will imagine the whole world is listening to me. I like to play the New Wave music that was coming out at the time when I look at his work, as I listen to jazz when I look at the art of the Impressionists.

I especially like the painting "Juicy Jungle." That unique world of fantasy you can admire, filled with joy. Kenny keeps that picture at home, but it should really be on permanent display somewhere.

Kenny was always sure of what he was doing. In the discussions we all had of the club's direction, he would join in with his characteristic jokes, sarcasm and contradictions, often even bordering on the malicious. His barbs, penetrating though they were, rarely made any of us angry or offended, for in our hearts we were like children, and anything could be said in this atmosphere of levity and indulgence.

In the beginning nobody took Kenny's pictures seriously. His fantasies were those of a small boy who liked to find things on the street, almost like Tom Sawyer. These he combined with his great imagination, and his love for animated cartoons. Old radios, all kinds of electronic parts and mechanical devices were incorporated into his work, giving them wonderful new forms and colors.

So I got one of his pictures to put in my restaurant. It hung between the counter and the kitchen door, and you could see it straight from the entrance. The painting consisted of cartoon creatures that swirled around a box that sported real radio knobs. The picture wasn't very large, but it attracted a lot of attention among the customers, who were always asking me who was that fantasy boy that created it.

Running a restaurant was very tiring for me and eventually I gave it up. I didn't have the strength to take the picture back, so I asked Ann Magnuson to take it to the club. I went to meet her at the restaurant, and there was Kenny. I told him I thought the club should keep the painting as a memento of those days, and he agreed. Then he went over to the picture and suddenly started to yell, "What happened? What's going on? Where's the button?" One of the buttons from the radio that had been glued onto the picture had fallen off. He started looking around, on the floor, under the counter, everywhere. No button. Kenny became furious. Oh, if I could only find out what company was responsible for making such weak glue, I would give them plenty of trouble.

Some time later I visited my friend Christine, who used to work for me in the restaurant. She had gotten her own place on 12th Street. So I asked her, "Do you recall that painter who came to my restaurant to take back his picture?"

"Oh, yes—that handsome, all-American boy with a kid's face that changed suddenly into the face of a rebel, a revolutionary. He was looking for the radio knob. He looked everywhere but he couldn't find it. He even tried to look for it in the pan where the pierogis were cooking, and in the drawer where we kept the money. He started throwing the money all around the restaurant. His eyes were throwing lightning bolts, flashing fire, and I was nailed to the spot with my eyes wide open, horrified, stricken. I don't know why the ceiling didn't fall on us, or why the world didn't end right then, but it was very close. And all because of that button.

"Then he grabbed the Heinz 57 ketchup and he started to pour it everywhere around him, whatever was close to his hands. After that he ran to the basement where, free of control, he finished his masterpiece. And you followed him. You, Stanley, you like to have interesting adventures, but you are also very cool and have a lot of self-control. Once a car drove into the front of the restaurant, destroying the window, the door and the front wall. Probably the driver was too hungry. I never saw such things except in the movies. And you pulled everything together and opened the restaurant in a few hours. And nobody even knew what had happened. Instead everybody noticed that there was a new, French-style restaurant in the village, open to the street. That evening was more crowded than ever, and there was a line in front. It was really so much fun to work with you, Stanley. Something always happens!"

"So, you know, Christine," I interrupted her speech, which may have never ended, "That painter is one of the best pop artists of the 20th century."

I never saw the painting again. But I will never forget its creator, who ran to the basement of the restaurant, pulling ketchup out of its case and pouring it everywhere—on the restaurant goods, the appliances, the fixtures. He poured ketchup on the flour, the canned goods, the produce. He poured it on the floor. His clothes came to resemble a painter's, with ketchup-paint all over him. As I watched him, suddenly he forgot where he was and, delighted, started to create fantastic designs. The basement became his studio. He treated the shelves as easels. The lettuce grew flowers, the cans of green peas looked like ice cream cones. The big paper bags sprouted funny faces of the kind I saw later in exhibitions at the Palladium nightclub.

The Coca-Cola, under Kenny's master hands, melded with the ketchup like it does with the pizza sauce at Stromboli's Pizza, creating a New Wave pop art fast food meal.

Then he took the broom and smeared the ketchup all over the floor, making a red carpet for the lucky first guest. But the lucky first guest was Anya the old cleaning lady, who did not deserve the red carpet treatment for what she did soon after, which was to destroy the artwork that the basement had become. But now Kenny was finished, relaxed and happy at last, and he took the painting and with great satisfaction ran with it to Club 57.

But even now I don't feel sorry that he took the picture, because I saw his best painting ever, painted with Heinz 57 Varieties Ketchup, full of ecstasy and fantasy, a fantastic panorama, which only a few people were lucky to have witnessed. Later I thought that maybe it showed the influence of Caravaggio when he threw things at his wild parties, or Jean-Michel Basquiat when he threw the paint on clothing at Fiorucci.

But I am sure he knows he belongs to my family, and he can show his feelings to us. He should also do a commercial for Heinz Ketchup.

As soon as he finished his masterpiece of art and vandalism, a victorious expression spread over his face and he said with a satisfied voice, "I am going to the club." He was already becoming popular in the art world. It happened so fast. I met him sometimes in Central Park with his little son, then at the Limelight club for a Halloween party organized by Ann Magnuson. His face was decorated with flourishes like the mask at his installation at the Whitney Biennial. He had an eye in the middle of his forehead, that stared at you together with his own unique psyche.

At the beginning they couldn't recognize me. My face was painted like an actor from the Peking Opera, and I wore a long kimono. "Hello," I called to Kenny and Ann.

"Hello, who are you?" asked Kenny. "Who's that?" asked Ann. Then they saw my wife, who is Chinese and wore a long gown and just a little makeup. I started to laugh. "Oh, Stanley," said Kenny, "When you smile I could recognize you from the back." We were like our masks. His was unconcerned with hiding, light-hearted and clear, made beautiful by romantic decoration, while mine was a disguise that covered my character and soul.

Soon after that I went to Rio de Janiero, and I was robbed by three hunters on the Copacabana Beach who held a knife to my throat. It reminded me of the picture of Kenny's that I like so much: "Juicy Jungle." In it you can see three masked men who look at you from behind a tree, lurking in the beauty of the tree and the happy world of nature. They are like the cats of darkness that assaulted me on the beach of Rio while I watched the most magnificent thunderstorm over the mountains of the city, interrupting me and pushing me from the world of fantasy, sending me to Earth, where bad nature, mostly of human origin, destroys human fantasy, dreams, imagination and wishes. These forces of evil, which destroy human plans, property, achievements and happiness, whether with hunger, poverty, war, hate, envy or deceit— you can also see in the paintings of Keith, Kenny and Jean-Michel.

At the time I was also promoting concerts at Irving Plaza. I thought that the concerts would lead to a creative environment for the kids who came there. But we were not the only ones using the hall, and so the management insisted that I restore the hall to its pristine condition after each event. So I had to paint the walls each time to cover up the footprints that found there way up its sides.

A popular meeting place inside Irving Plaza was the ladies' room. Not only was it full of beautiful girls, it also had comfortable couches— and very attractive walls for using Magic Markers. The walls were soon painted all over by various graffitists. Mornings after, the wall paint and rags had much to say about it. My house manager John Richard bore the brunt of my anger at having to do this extra work. So one evening during the concert he called me over and said, "Stanley, that guy is painting graffiti on the wall in the girls' toilet!"

I snorted angrily. I watched the young black man drawing on the wall, when suddenly he realized he had been spotted, and he ran upstairs into the concert hall. I was already tired from dancing, and from running up and down the stairs, but I followed him, and found him sitting in the back, right where Sid Vicious had been sitting the week before, acting as if he hadn't done anything. I bent over to the boy and said, "Can you give me your Magic Marker please?" He didn't say anything. He took the marker from his pocket and delivered it to me so calmly and coolly, and looked at me with eyes sparkling like two stars, the most innocent man in the world. So winsome and winning was his face, he seemed to be forgiving me my question and behavior. If anyone ever conquered me with his deportment, it was he, Jean-Michel Basquiat. He gave me the gift of his smile, a smile that even Mona Lisa could be jealous of. It contained so much cheer and good humor toward the world, and mischief as well. "I forgive you your badgering, now get lost!" he seemed to be saying.

I brought him a bottle of beer, wordlessly begging him to disregard my indelicacy. He took the bottle, giving me the smile again, that said, "Thank you for your apology in giving me the beer." That was my first strange conversation with him without words, my introduction to Jean-Michel Basquiat.

His Magic Marker sat a long time on my desk, reminding me of him and the way we met. Sometimes inanimate objects seem to be alive, don't they?

Jean-Michel became friends with Kenny and Keith, but he also cruised around more, in the clubs and the streets, looking for new friends and adventures. He was rather a lonely man, not really having a harbor for his personal life. Perhaps it was this that led him to abuse drugs.

Keith used the idiom of graffiti, Kenny his cartoon imagination. But Jean-Michel belonged to the street. His art contained everything from graffiti to icons to slogans to naïve depictions. He didn't attend art school. He created his own school, made up of newspapers, magazines, observations of characters he met on the street. All of this ended up in his pictures.

And then came the day when my mother and I entered St. Peter's Church for his memorial mass. All his friends and collaborators had come to pay tribute to his life and art. In front of the altar his face peered from a poster at the assembled mourners, full of the charisma unique to him. I recalled the day I saw him outside an art gallery in Soho. Nobody would let him show then; but the street was his showroom. Still nobody really knows him.

He was sitting on the sidewalk, selling T-shirts he had painted. He had used symbols known only to himself; faces, lines, spots and words describing the conflict between man and his life. I was just going with my mom to some art gallery. I noticed him and I stopped to look at him for a while. Then I said, "Hi, Michel, I haven't seen you in the club for a long time." So of course he answered in his teasing way, "I haven't seen you in Soho for a long time. I must earn some money for my apartment."

"I would like to see you sometime, and your pictures as well," I told him. I looked straight into his dazzling black eyes. He knew I was looking longer than usual. "Do you want to see my eyes or my pictures?" he asked. "Both," I answered. "Some people make me feel good when I'm around them, and you're one of those. Some call it chemistry."

"But you never have time; you're constantly working, going to Irving Plaza or to court. Do you really like judges that much? Everybody says you help people like me. I wish you would be my brother. I am looking for a brother, and in church the priest says we are all brothers. Maybe it's true, maybe it's just communication that's difficult." He rarely talked this much, or this seriously.

"I am your brother," I said, "Even if you didn't know it. I have so much to do, I need 36 hours a day, and now with you, one hour more. Come to the club tomorrow, and we can talk about our friendship."

"You'd better give me my Magic Marker back. I'm not so rich that I can buy a new one, and you rich people like to steal from the poor. But I am very generous. Here, have something extra," he said, passing me one of his T-shirts.

"Oh, yea, give it to me, and take this," I said, giving him $20.

"I don't want it, but I'll take it to buy new paint to paint the club, if nobody spies on me like you did at Irving Plaza. Anyway, it is not enough. The T-shirts are very expensive, because I am the number one painter on this sidewalk." Then I gave him some more money, and he slapped me five with great cheer. "Oh, yeah! Actually, I wanted to revenge you for the drink you gave me the first time we met. You know I was very angry at you like I was angry at the whole world. But you got me that time, by your manners. You are a very interesting person. And if you buy one more T-shirt I will give you more compliments."

"Oh, no," I said. "I gave you a drink because you gave me the marker." We forgot about reality, and started to play a teasing game. We were laughing. "And the shirt," I added, "I will wear to let you know how close to my heart is your painting." As I left him I waggled my finger at him and, smiling, eyes shining as always, he returned the gesture, grimacing at my mother as if to say, How can you stand to accompany such a man?

When I am looking at the art of most artists I admire, I think of the kind of music I would like to hear at the same time. But with Basquiat, whose work has such drama, I just want silence. The only music I could possibly pair with Basquiat is Beethoven's Ninth Symphony, whose dramatic impact his work matches.

"Mother," I asked at St. Peter's, "Do you remember Jean-Michel?" She looked at me, then at his face on the poster at the front, and tears flowed over her cheeks, and fell on her knees and wrinkled hands. I didn't have tears in my eyes, I'm sorry, they were invisible …

Whuh …

I had to take a little break from writing, to get a breath of air. Something was choking me. And I don't like to write on wet paper …

One day a boy with a hot heart and a smiling face came to the club. His name was Tseng Kwong Chi. Born in Hong Kong, he wandered across the world and ended up in New York, to meet the most friendly man in New York, Keith Haring. Keith was always hunting for the ideal noble friend, and in Tseng Kwong Chi his choice was perfect. Haring grabbed him off the street and brought him immediately to the club. There he instantly became the photographer of the New Wave generation, capturing the life of Club 57 and all its inhabitants, including Dan Friedman, John Sex, Drew Straub, Samantha McEwen, Bruno Schmidt and others, as well as the previously mentioned "big three" painters. This group began to coalesce as friends and also as a philosophical and artistic school that started out in the East Village and began making its mark in New York art society, first in Soho and soon after in the museums and galleries uptown. Characteristic of an artistic movement, everything bloomed rapidly like flowers in the spring, and many in this group suddenly became famous.

I tried to rent the upper church hall for an art studio, to give them an opportunity to stay and work together. But by now the church wanted a lot of money, and the plan failed. So this art laboratory of Club 57 went their separate ways, some, like Haring and Basquiat, working with Warhol at the Factory, others traveling to galleries and museums in Tokyo, Berlin and all over the world. It was time for me to say goodbye to them. The kids got married to fame and the mature world, who gave them a warm welcome.

During Christmas time 1994 I received a beautiful picture and poem made by the hands of my 8-year-old cousin Esterka Brudek. It was to thank me for the Christmas party I made for my entire family in New York. She is very talented, so I told her she'd better cultivate it. I told her mother, "Anna, don't you see, look how much fantasy of form and color it has." I hope she takes my advice and helps the girl to be the Angel of Human Achievement.

When I came home I said to my mother, "You like art and painting so much, you visit all the greatest galleries and museums of the world. Why don't you do at least one picture in your life?" I took some markers and tried to give them to her.

"Don't bother me," she said. "You know that in my life, besides putting the wax on the floor of Club 57, I never did any painting. You are malicious, wanting me to be one of the Club 57 artists. All I have painted was butter on slices of bread."

"There was a lot of art in it," I interrupted her. And then I reminded her of Kenny's ketchup painting. "Try," I said. "Paint at least one flower for Jean-Michel."

"No!" she replied decidedly. But it seems the name of Jean-Michel melted her heart. And she took the markers and painted a green sprig with small red flowers on it. And she left the room with wet eyes. I put this in a frame and titled it "The Flower for Jean."

Perhaps you can paint flowers for somebody you love. If you can't do it with a brush, at least do it with your imagination. Or start to think about your life, the best, most colorful dream and picture you ever knew. This memoir is my picture of the art of art and the art of friendship, and the art of creation.

Little Nicole, whom I spoke of earlier, will be gone from my life someday, but now she is my youngest friend, and I enjoy her brightening my life. I recall that green bird whistle which she lost like my youth, almost gone, like a colorful picture, like my colorful dream, like Proust's "Remembrance Of Things Past," which evokes the same emotion: the search backward for one's life.

Chapter Twelve

John Sex

Look! How a bird lies tangled in a net,
So fasten'd in her arms Adonis lies;
Pure shame and aw'd resistance made him fret,
Which bred more beauty in his angry eyes.

---Shakespeare

So, here we are again. Sex. Also John, who was whistling ... I opened the window and looked down at him. He called me to join him for lunch. He lived on the next block over on St. Mark's Place and it was easy for him to pick me up on his way to Leshko's restaurant. And in a minute we were sitting and ordering scrambled eggs with bacon, home fries and coffee.

The waiter is named Terry. He puts down two glasses of water with his mouth hanging open like the whole world belongs to him. Probably he knows us, because at once he says, "I play the electric organ. I have my own band with a bunch of friends. I wish I could play Club 57."

"I know somebody there," I answer, "But first I would like to know how you play."

"You can stop by my apartment if you're not afraid of roaches and mice. I live on 6th Street and Avenue B."

"OK," I tell him, "Prepare some songs and I'll visit you in a few days." Terry's eyes sparkle and he starts to run around the restaurant double-time.

"Did you sleep well?" I ask John.

"Very well. I didn't even have erotic dreams, which doesn't happen too often. But my stomach's growling chased me from my bed. I even stopped playing with the 'toy.' It was almost 12 noon."

"Aren't you oversexed?"

"Probably. I think that all my life I've been interested in eroticism. I can't stop thinking about it, the delight of it. Sometimes I look at my friends and other people around me, and I wonder, Do they ever think like I do? They're always talking about something else. Or maybe it's just me who's that way. I'm too shy to ask anybody else about it."

"But how do you feel about it? Do you like that feeling?"

John smiles his very wide smile. Knowing him for so long, I feel I can ask him this. "You know, Stan, friends and people I know spoil me. They see me as a sex object, not only because they say, 'You're a cute boy,' but they really like me, they want to be my friends and more. But I actually feel comfortable with that. I like it."

"You live in a tolerant society," I tell him. "When I was a teenager in Poland, my friends and I were highly controlled by our families and society. There wasn't any good information on what to do with that always-hard 'banana.' I was too shy to talk about it to anybody, even when I wanted to talk. Mostly I got a headache and a wet dream. I was mad, that fate gave me such a thing to suffer with. Especially when in catechism they told you that even to think about it was the worst thing in the world, unimaginably shameful. And it was just as bad at school as in church. I always wondered how my other friends could stand it—or how the priests could control themselves."

"How do you see it now?" asks John.

"I haven't found any better solution than just masturbating. Fighting with sexual feelings gave me some kind of way to separate feelings of love and sex. I love many people and I don't even tell them. Some kind of Platonic love. I put the sexual feeling into refined, sublimated love. But now I've elevated sex to the highest level. Vulgar sex annoys me."

John pulls his toast from his mouth energetically and a sneaky smile crosses his lips. Then he says:

"You know that in some religions in Greece, India and Indochina, eroticism played central roles. And they were happy societies. They treated sex as sacred. We have so many religions in America—let's start one more."

"Very interesting," I answer. But you need at least ten people."

"No problem. I can think of several kids right away."

"I'm afraid, though. I know one group of twelve friends that did that. And one rejected his master, and another betrayed him."

But we kept talking.

The coffee was good. Terry poured a few refills. And each time his mouth hung open it was as if to say. "I'm a nice boy. Don't forget about me."

John and I go back to my apartment. My mother comes over too. Now we'll count the money from last night's gig at Irving Plaza. My mother figures that after the James Brown show, I can give her back the money I borrowed from her. But now I have to pay to build two new bars inside the club, and put up soundproofing too.

In the middle of the livingroom lies a stack of money, waiting for us to count and sort it. Mom counts the hundreds; John counts the singles. I count the quarters.

"When will you go see your mother?" Mom asks John.

"I haven't visited her for a long time. I'd like to see her. I haven't entirely lost the habit of it. But I live with my girlfriend now. Also, I see you both at the club almost every day. It makes me feel like you are my family.

"Anyway," he asks Mom, "How come you still look like you're twenty? Where do you find the energy to dance to rock music at Irving Plaza?"

"I was trained as a teacher," Mom replies. It is coded in my psyche to be with the young. And I must play my little role to match the atmosphere and play the fool sometimes."

"How do you like James Brown?" he asks her.

"I really like him. He was such a gentleman, and so modest. He not only kissed both my cheeks, but he invited me to visit him in his house. His family, especially his mother, who prepared his clothing, is very charming. His mother looks at him like he's a saint. Sometimes you can make friends very fast.

"And the show was great, the hall was packed. The kids were so crazy about him. I'm sure there will be enough money now."

"Oh, sure," John says. "But, you know, it's not so great living on the same street with Stanley. As soon as he sees me he starts thinking about how to give me some work to do."

"You complain you don't have money. And now you complain he's giving you work."

"Just kidding. I hope he'll make a jacket for me with these bills. I never saw so much money before in my life."

"How did Stanley get you?" Mom asks.

"By mistake," John jokes. "I saw all these beautiful girls in front of the club and I thought, 'So many nice girls but no boys.' This was Anna and her girlfriends from the Ladies Auxiliary. So I said, 'Hello, beauties!' And they answered, 'Hello, cutie! We dream about you, and here you are.' So I became a club member. The first work they gave me to do was to scrape the floor. No sex at all. Can you imagine?"

"That's horrible," says my Mother, laughing, "that you had to suffer like that."

"But later they gave me better work," John continues. "Like painting the bar black. After that they caught two other boys and told them to take their clothes off. One was Kenny Scharf and the other was Shawn McQuate. And some black boy who was so cute too, but I don't remember his name. I didn't even know that I had become Club 57's Chippendale boy."

"Why did Stanley ask you to help count the money?" Mom asks. "Because you live close by, or because you caught his eye and he has a lot of laughs with you? Or are you a very honest boy?"

"He likes to look into people's eyes. When he looks at you and he likes you, you have to belong to him. Did he have to have all the toys when he was a kid?"

"He said once that not too many people are honest," said Mom. "But he isn't himself. Once he confessed he stole things from other little boys when he was a kid. Now he can't sleep because of it."

These were the kind of conversations we had with John, who likes to laugh at everybody.

John McLaughlin came from Long Island with his girlfriend Wendy Andreiev and got an apartment on St. Mark's Place, on the same block as the club. When he attended the School of Visual Arts on 23rd Street he met a few friends whom he brought to the club as well. He was a talented boy and, like Ann Magnuson, enthusiastic about all art events.

Ironic, sarcastic and very witty, their brains open wide in all directions, they knew each other's minds and they were just what I needed.

John participated in almost every event the club produced, which we did almost every evening. His mind was an open book in which you could read his soul, a soul of a frank, sincere little boy, who could never lie or say anything to hurt someone. Once, after his money-counting job was over, he said to me: "Stan, you truly put me on a trial of strength. How can you give such a poor boy so much money to count? One time when you went to the toilet I wanted to take 20 bucks. It was a lot of money for me at the time. I didn't take it. But I didn't feel too good for a whole day after that. I was very angry at you for putting me up to that. I still don't know what kind of person you really are. You believed in me, and in Ann, Susan, Tom, Dale Ashmun, and the others. You won us over. How did you do it?"

John became a pillar of the club, along with Ann.

Later he met Shawn McQuate, and they became inseparable friends, though only for a year. Together they organized many shows, and if they weren't together they were in a bad mood. They had a friendship like David and Jonathan from the Bible.

John's first successful art show, called "Acts of Live Art," took place in April of 1980. There he gave full range to his fantasies, of which he had an inexhaustible supply. He often finished with a sexual parody he himself enacted onstage. Most memorable was one he did as a matador, fighting an imaginary bull, that paralyzed us with laughter.

I know of only one country where books can be considered smut: the USA. That's how it happened that John and Keith Haring found a book entitled "The Sex Guide To Married Life." So they read it aloud from the steps of the club. Everyone jeered, especially when Keith confusedly recited its "description of the typical homosexual."

This reading opened the door to a never-ending discussion of sex, love and personal friendship. From that time on the ice was broken among the club members, and led to a strong and intimate bond that embraced all in a cloak of sexual tolerance. Suddenly everyone discovered that they could be friends regardless of their differences, that no one would deride them.

Meanwhile, John had become a full-fledged sex symbol—not

only at the club, but throughout the East Village. I booked John for a performance at Irving Plaza, opening for Joy Ryder's band.

Joy had a very refined personality, and I was a little embarrassed when John did his parody of a strip tease which, though it was a parody, the gay members of audience took very seriously, stuffing dollar bills down his shorts. I thought the show would be more artistic, perhaps more along the lines of Lady Bug's strip act for the New Wave Vaudeville show, which incorporated classical ballet moves. But the public liked it anyway, and I always had to forgive John. Besides, wasn't Club 57 an artistic laboratory, with satire and parody at its very base?

As I mentioned, John attended SVA, and graphic art and painting weren't strange to him. He started doing posters for the Irving Plaza events. He had a show of his posters at the Second Wave Gallery in the East Village. After that he started making posters of his own persona, that of a sex idol.

I wanted to help him out financially, so I sent him to a bartender's school. But after a few lessons he came to me and said, "I won't go to that fuckin' school anymore. They don't teach anything special at all, not even how to do the drinks right."

"Then how can I help you?" I asked.

"I'll try to be a sex star, the way kids like to see me."

"Do what you want," I told him. "I can't see much of a future in it, not to my way of thinking." So John started to do all kinds of shows, not only at my club but at other night spots as well. The time had come when the Club 57 crew had started to think about their financial and professional futures.

John had also become close friends with Jean-Michel Basquiat. They started producing their own postcards as a way to reach the marketplace. It was a very brief attempt.

You could see the differences in their personalities during the Elvis Memorial Party in August 1980. A small fire caused by a shirt getting caught in the air conditioner set off an unheard-of panic. John was the first to the door, yelling "Get out of my way!" But not Jean-Michel. He didn't even shift from his corner, where he was smoking pot. In his life's experience this was a small danger.

Meanwhile Tom cut off the electricity and I choked out the flames with a rag. Jean-Michel passed his joint to me, saying, "Take a puff."

I was unaccustomed to the marijuana smoke and I coughed. "They don't take good care of you here," observed Jean-Michael. Now you're choking. But thanks for not chasing me out of the club anymore. It's a very funny place."

Tom Scully took a few steps nearer to me and said, "Susan called the Fire Department, I don't know why. But I'm telling you, the spirit of Elvis came to the club, and that's where the sparks came from."

Sure, the house didn't burn down because the altar of Elvis made by Kathy was in the middle of the floor.

"This kid," said Tom, pointing to Jean-Michel, "was praying to him. Now you see how it works. Hallelujah and glory to the spirit of Elvis!"

And he ran out with his new idea, where the participants of the party had not let go of their drinks.

That makes me recall a song from my old hiking club that we used to sing in the mountains:

Hallelujah
Glory to God
For church was burned
But the tavern was not

"Come with me," I said to the overly pious Jean-Michel, and I pulled him into the street where, dressed up in rock'n'roll clothes, Tseng Kwong Chi was doing his Elvis impression.

Then the fire trucks came, along with a few cops. Added to the displaced partygoers, they caused a lot of bypassers to stop. And so we all paid homage to Elvis together.

John Sex, as proud as if he had stayed to the end and extinguished the fire himself, posed with the firemen for photos. And Tom and Drew proclaimed the first official miracle of the club's history.

One day, as I went to have my usual lunch at the Zen Café, looking at the small pictures of potatoes someone had painted on the street, I noticed a commotion in front of 65 St. Mark's Place. The boys and girls were milling around, searching for something. In the middle was John, who seemed to be directing the search. I asked him what he was doing.

"Delilah is gone," John cried. "My best friend, after Shawn, has left me Besides, I need her for my performances."

"Did you give her enough mice?" I queried.

"I gave her plenty of mice. But she's an unfaithful snake. Not only that, she's always trying to bite my cock."

Finally the cops came, just in time to hear the lady who lived one story below John scream that the huge boa constrictor had taken up residence on her carpet. Guarding it was a very frightened orange cat whose hair stuck out like a bottle brush.

"Goodbye, John," I said. "Next time don't run around naked in your apartment. You must have scared her."

John stuck out his tongue and kissed Delilah. I went to Zen.

After the book-reading incident, discussions about sexuality became more frequent, and more pointed.

"What you think about the sexual trends in America, Stanley?" asked Ann.

"The first time I touched on it was in Greenwich Village. Not long ago you could see streakers there, boys and girls running naked. But after a while nobody paid attention to them. Now it's all onstage."

At Irving Plaza the girls started running naked up to the stage, grabbing the soloists. It was more innocent than bad, but I banned it anyway for security reasons, and even posted an extra guard on the stage to control the situation.

But when I first came to New York, nude shows were the hit of Broadway. One was called "Let My People Come." The show treated sexual behavior and orientations in a well-mannered, esthetic way. I myself never use dirty words. But at that show I accepted it. The actors were naked, the music from traditional to more boisterous.

The public was mostly straight and accepted the show with pretty good applause. There was another brave sexual show on Fourteenth Street, "Boys, Boys, Boys." Those things are history now. I was fooling around town, attending different clubs and different art levels, knowing more of the tree of good and bad. But I didn't eat the apple yet.

One time John asked me suddenly, "Did you ever have sex with a boy, Stan?" I didn't answer him. Instead I punched his chest and we started to fight. We fell on the floor in the club. Nobody was there except Ann. She was scared at what was going on. I was sitting on top of John. Ann said, "Leave him alone, you will smash his chest!" Of course the fighting was just another case of "Friendly fire," which is why Johnny yelled, "I wanted to be on top of him, I wanted!"

"Boys will be boys," said Ann, and poured the soda which was in her hand onto us.

"Why did you ask such a question?" I asked John after a while.

"Because I became more attractive to girls, and not only girls. Sometimes I am in an embarrassing situation because I like them, and many of them wanted to have an adventure with me. Life became more interesting, attractive and dramatic. It isn't so easy to be a sex symbol. I can't practice sex when I want, and with whom I want, like James Dean or David Bowie, because of my fame. I am not as famous as them. But I can do it because it is my passion."

"It's very difficult to control our strange fancies," I said, "Not only for you. It isn't easy to be mature. We constantly have to learn how to control ourselves, not only in sex. The more you are in control, the more you are a human being. Be careful, kid. Try to be with people whom you love, not just anybody. We have many dreams, sometimes very perverted. Sometimes the dreams come true, but mostly not. They just have to be dreams, that's all. Too much strawberry ice cream instead of bread can cause stomach problems."

"You like to use expressions. It helps," said John. We were looking at each other for a long time. We understood that love is more than sex, much more.

So, John "went to the world," along with the others. The delusive world of fame. I received a postcard from Japan: "Stanley, the Japanese are very interesting people and very intelligent. Our New Wave Act was received with open arms. This is the first time I've been so far from New York. Ann, Keith and Tseng are with me. We are having lots of adventures. See you soon on St. Mark's. I will pay for lunch. Regards from everybody, John."

Later we had that lunch. I had recently introduced John to Grace, whom I met in Shanghai. "I am so glad you started to enjoy the world," said John. "You went everywhere, and even brought back a wife."

"So, I like exocentrism, exoticism, and Asian women. Anyway, isn't she pretty?"

"Sure," answered John, "and much smarter than you. She would probably never let those geniuses from Irving Plaza close the show at the same moment you had the best New York venue in your hands.

"I'm not sorry I don't have anything to do with them," I answered. "I am sorry only because I lost the best people, the Copelands. I dreamed they would be my friends. I am sorry that I could not make dreams come true for those who helped me to conquer New York and make this world better. I took their best years, and wound the clock of their lives to run better and more accurately. Life is time. If I didn't do it well, I hope they will forgive me. Experience is a hard teacher when it comes to manipulators. And what are you going to do now?" I asked John.

"An art program with Ann. I have many orders for performances. I also sing and play guitar. When I started to copy Presley and Liberace I became more popular and attractive at New York clubs. Maybe there will be TV and films, who knows. One time you told me about true friendship. I think I now have someone who is really my friend. More mature than Shawn."

"Are we going to have lunch again?" I asked.

"I think I owe you more than lunch, Stanley," he said.

October 1982. The phone is ringing. It's John. "Tonight there is a dance party at the club. Ira said it is a closed party and suggested I go somewhere else for a good time. Why? I want to go to 57 with you. Wait for me at ten at the door, OK?"

"OK," I answered, even though I was tired of spending every night at the club.

At ten I entered the club with John. Little Karen at the door smiled and asked, "did you see Ira's performance?"

"Oh, yea," I answered, even though I had not. We stood near the bar, drank Bud, listen to 60's rock'n'roll, and …

One hundred ravishing girls, forgetting about the world as they dance in a shake-up rhythm. I feel as though I am at the Metropolitan Ballet, watching Tchaikovsky's "Swan Lake," except the music is different.

I watched them dance, entranced. It seemed as if they had transmitted that music to their white arms, pretty legs, round hips and bouncing breasts. It was a long time since I had seen so many exquisitely joyful girls, and so much enthusiasm. Some spiritual bond. I got the same feeling when the Fleshtones had their first gig here in 1978.

John's pants are straining and his eyes are sparkling like two lanterns. "Stanley, aren't we in Eden already? Look at that black-haired girl. Do you see her white neck, which I would like to kiss, did you see these eyes, lips and breast which I want to ..."

The music suddenly changed. The row of dancing girls divided and Ira emerged and began to dance with them. Their dresses were encrusted with shiny sequins, hair curled and cheeks made up with a lot of paint like those at the "Cats" show on Broadway. Ira, his hips undulating, is doing a Hawaiian dance. His face is painted pretty heavy too. On his head is a wig. He probably wanted to be more beautiful than the two girls near him. The three twisted to the center of the hall and did a belly dance. "Dany," I said to the bartender, "Give John another beer. We'll have to cool him off or I'll have to throw him into a cold shower."

"How do you like the party?" asked Dany.

"Of course, we need more parties like this. Not too many boys, just me and John. And the girls have class." On the wall is a poster of Virginia Woolf, looking down at us. Judy Garland is singing. What kind of party is this?" I asked Dany. "Is it a shower?"

"Actually, " said Dany, "This is Lesbian Night."

John looked at me and then at the girls, then at Ira, who was now dancing the can-can, and said, "From today I am a Lesbian too."

I am at home and the telephone rings. It is John.

"Stan, did you read today's New York Times? My picture's in it. I was at one of Liberace's parties. He's a cool guy. He got to like me. And he speaks Polish. Not with me, of course. I told him about you, that you founded Club 57 and your name is Stifihasky."

"Strychacki," I corrected him. "Why don't you learn another language already? I know four. My name is for people who know more than a few letters of the alphabet."

"I'll forgive you for having such a long name, but don't criticize me, or I'll tell your mother that you're a ..."

"—You can tell her whatever you want, just continue the story."

"I invited Liberace to your restaurant for pierogis. He agreed to come on the condition that the meal was on the house, because he's broke. He had to give Donald Trump his last penny for that party.

"He said he was so glad you like Michelangelo. He has a copy of Adam from the Sistine Chapel painted on his ceiling."

"I didn't know he was so religious, John. Give him a picture of 'Saint John Sex of the East Village' so he can put that on his wall."

"You see," says John, "Not every Pole is a tough guy, which is what I thought after knowing you. I just can't stop laughing when you told me that the crew from Irving Plaza hid in the basement after the first punk rock show. They were so afraid of all those chains, safety pins and painted hair, and you were terrified that the crystal chandeliers would come crashing down from the ceiling."

"So, blabbermouth, what other lies did you tell to Liberace?"

"Of course, I told him you were an attractive and intelligent man. But he shook his head and sighed, said he couldn't believe such humbug."

"But he wants to come eat pierogis?"

"Just because he's broke. He also wants to buy my apartment. He can have Ann's instead. She's moving to Hollywood after 'Making Mr. Right' comes out." Ann's first lead in a Hollywood film came in "Mr. Right."

So I went out and bought the Times. Looking at me from the page was the same smiling John, the all-American boy with bright blue eyes and his famous stiff, foot-high blond pompadour.

I remember my last happy moment with John. One day he asked me, "Stanley, why, when I am asking you some questions, instead of answering you punch my chest?"

"If you swear you won't tell anybody I'll tell you."

"I swear!"

"I'm the worst pervert in the world. but I grew up in a prudish society. So I am also a hypocrite. For me it is easier to stay that way and not give an honest answer."

"You are not the worst, but the best!" John's voice rose higher. "You are not a hypocrite, but a fuckin' crazy punk!"

I tried to punch him, but he was too fast for me. He tripped me. I fell, and he was on top of me. He was punching me everywhere, but being careful not to hurt me, yelling "You're a fucking punk!" and "I love you!" But this time Ann wasn't around to pour water on us.

Chapter Thirteen

The East Village Eye

"Ogenki Desuka," I said to the wooden Buddha in the window of the Zen Café.

"How are you?" answered the waitress, who didn't realize that I was talking to the Indian prince. As I was looking at her, I couldn't tell if the Buddha answered me, but I give you my word that he bowed to me, and it wasn't just the shadow from the opening door. It made me think of Princess Diana, the way he went out into the world looking for wisdom, truth and the paths to goodness, as young people have done for thousands of years.

Like this sensitive, acute gentleman Leonard Abrams, who will be here in a minute to have dinner with me and spend some time recalling the years he spent (as did I) burnishing the cultural landscape of New York.

He started as the advertising supplement editor of the Gramercy Herald, and within six months, after meeting crazy dreamers like himself (and me), he started his own magazine: the East Village Eye.

He started in 1979, like a gypsy, moving his office from Ludlow Street to 3rd Street to St. Mark's Place in the course of one year. He started with $100 in his pocket, ripped jeans and a head full of ideas. He went around Manhattan meeting and enlisting others into a circle of like-minded individuals with a common view of the neighborhood in which they ate, slept and searched for a new worldview. How often they had to cut themselves off from their families, national origins, religions and political and moral roots to build their own philosophy of common coexistence and creation.

Early key members of the Eye included Richard Fantina, a writer who also supplied the crucial and then very expensive typography secretly from his job at a typesetting shop; Celest-Monique Lindsey, a longtime friend who became a valuable contributor; Irene Stepash, an editor at Sexual Medicine magazine who was the magazine's first Associate Editor in her spare time; Chris Kohlhoefer, the avant-garde artist from Dusseldorf who became the first Art Director; and Richard Hell, the punk rocker whose career as a writer began as author of the "Slum Journal," an Eye exclusive, and who made sure the world would know that he "invented" punk, by use of his column.

Then came David Katz, a wicked satirist who made fun of our hypocritical society; Sylvia Falcon, a very pessimistic woman who always discovered the brightest young artists; Carlo McCormich and Walter Robinson, who together put the "scene" in "East Village Art Scene," a big feature of the East Village at the time that has since disappeared; Brien Coleman and Valerie Van Cleve, whose astrology column was twisted but always true; James Marshall, whose rock'n'roll column always remembered the great legends; Beauregard Houston-Montgomery, whose gossip column always created a huge fuss around town ... the list goes on and on, and I can't even list them all, because, as Mr. Abrams tells me, once the magazine got going, about 50 people had some kind of work in each issue. With all these people, the Eye went everywhere, like the sound of the bells of St. Stan.

There was hardly a concert, art exhibition, poetry reading or party that someone from the Eye didn't go to. The Eye saw most of the energetic life of the East Village, the punks, the musicians, the painters and the poets, the organizations and the clubs—all the people and things that had an influence on the city's life.

After a few years of hard struggle, the arts institutions joined the nightclubs in supporting the Eye with advertisements, along with the many small private art galleries that sprang up in the East Village like mushrooms after a rainstorm, and the Eye became the premier independent/ "underground" arts magazine in New York.

But not only in New York. People started reading the Eye all over the world. To advertise this fact, they started a feature called "Far-Out Eye," in which readers outside of New York took pictures of themselves holding the magazine. The picture taken farthest away from the East

Village was the winner, and that person got a free subscription, and his or her picture in the paper. People sent pictures of themselves on camels in the Sahara, in a bullring in Spain, even from the back streets of Seoul.

Naturally, the Eye often had information about Club 57, especially since one of its busiest—and thirstiest—columnists, Tony Love, was great friends with John Sex and Ira Abramowitz, both key figures of Club 57, as the reader knows by now. Tony would use his promises of fame to get free food and drinks, and he got plenty of them from me, Ann and Ira. Leonard once said that to find out where the most generous bar managers worked, all you had to do was read his column. But he also supplied what he promised: Tony wrote about them all, large and small, and many people who are famous today were first written about in Tony's column.

But it wasn't always peaceful around the Eye office. One famous incident occurred in which Richard Hell was very upset about the treatment of some drawings he submitted to go with his column. Well, they weren't just any drawings. They were drawings of his penis. One of the art directors at that time, Bobby Kern, drew the printer's marks right on the drawings—a clear sign of disrespect of Richard's private property. What caused him to do such a thing? Was it disapproval? Envy? We may never know.

What we know is that Richard went to the office to pick up the drawings, accompanied only by writer Sybil Walker, and when he saw the blue lines on his prized work, he went crazy (just like Kenny Scharf in Chapter Eleven, "The Painter"), and "beat up" the office. He threw chairs and papers around and then stormed out in a huff.

Well, that's his version. Actually, Miss Walker later said that the reason he beat up the office was that she told him his drawings weren't very good. Or maybe it was the subject matter she insulted ...

That reminds me of another funny story I heard about the Eye. It was Tony's birthday, and Tony invited the whole Eye crew to the apartment of his girlfriend, where Tony was living, "rent-free," at the time. Tony was bragging a lot about this arrangement, so Leonard decided to play a trick on him. Sylvia brought a bottle of cheap white wine that nobody wanted from an art opening. In her typical pessimistic style, she offered it with many warnings about its quality. But before she could set it down, Leonard grabbed it and wrote "$22.50" on it with a grease pencil. Then he showed it to Tony. "Look, Tony!" he said with great enthusiasm, "Steve {Hager, now Editor of High Times} just made a lot of money selling a story. See how much he spent on that wine?" Tony just gave a wink.

Later they opened up the bottle and Tony took a big sip. Then, with a big smile, he said "Yeah, that's what they're drinking on Park Avenue tonight!"

Tony suffered greatly when his friends told him the truth, but he wasn't too mad to be the band leader at the Mr. & Ms. East Village Eye Pageant at the Mudd Club.

I wasn't there, but I overheard a conversation between Tony Love and John Sex that explained the whole thing:

Tony and John were sitting in Club 57 watching Ira talk to Ann. I think maybe Tony got jealous because he turned to John and said, "Do you see that wiseguy Ira giving Ann the 'charm treatment'?"

"Yes, I see him," John answered.

"Well, I have a story to tell about him."

"Then speak up."

"I can't. My throat's too dry."

"I'll bring you a Bud."

"Don't joke with me, please. For a sore throat, Heineken is the only answer."

"I'm broke. And Ann won't give me a Heineken."

"Go to Stanley. He doesn't know that Ann already gave you a beer."

"I prefer not hearing the story," answered John, "than lying to them."

"This is not lying. This is a simple, small, gentle game, and if you still feel bad about it, tomorrow when you come to the club, don't drink the beer."

John went to the bar and said, "Stan, may I have a Heineken? I will pay you tomorrow." And he returned to the table with Tony's beer, saying, "So what is it, now?"

Tony took a big gulp and replied, "Ira has won the title of 'Mr. East Village Eye.' According to the East Village Eye, Ira is the most handsome and talented man in the East Village. Now Ann is admiring him. But she's not wearing glasses, so maybe she thinks the same thing."

"I think only Picasso could capture his beauty," answered John. "I already know about the title, and the decision to give it to Ira was based on his craftiness. Besides, you think I don't know he's singing in your band?"

"All I know is he won, and for that he's getting a free weekend at the Carleton Arms Hotel, dinner at Leshko's, free invitations to all the clubs, and a pack of subway tokens."

"So what?" said John. "I prefer Brenda Bergman. She's a lot sexier."

We were all very proud of Ira, who shared his award with Brenda, who was chosen to be Ms. East Village Eye. Ira impressed the judges with his "Beatnik who commutes from Connecticut" performance. Both winners got their pictures in the Eye's centerfold, and Ira tried to sell me the tokens later.

The Eye crew always had lots of parties. It seemed they couldn't do anything without making a party to celebrate it. They had a party each year for Christmas, they had a party for their 5th anniversary, and they had parties to celebrate their successes and they had parties to raise money when they were broke. The party I remembered best, naturally, was the one at Irving Plaza, when the Eye was very young. My favorite acts were Jackie Curtis, the famous transvestite chanteuse, and Susin Shox, a New Wave band that will always be remembered by their remake of the country hit, "Tammy."

The other big "show" happened in the Ladies' Room. Inside was a big, full-length mirror, and in front of it was a very drunk punk girl, holding a bottle of beer in her hand. As she stared at herself into the mirror, a very bright idea slowly came into her head.

"Think I can break this mirror?" she asked her friend, another very drunk "punkette."

"I dunno," the friend answered. "Why don't you try?" These were the encouraging words the girl was waiting for. In another second, the mirror's glass was flying everywhere.

And in a few minutes after that, Alex, that "bad apple" who ran Irving Plaza for me for a short time, ran up to Leonard and screamed: "Look what your audience did to my club! That will cost $100 to fix!" Leonard, who just felt bad about it and didn't know it was not his responsibility, quickly paid the $100. Later, Alex told me what happened—except the part about him getting $100. So guess who fixed the mirror? That's right—me.

This reminiscing with Leonard gave me great satisfaction. Like myself, he really liked these streets and the people walking on them. The East Village would not have been the same, if it wasn't for him and his enthusiastic "misfit" friends.

"We started our magazine with 28 pages, and it went eventually to 68 pages. I like the earlier ones the best, I guess because everything was so new and everyone was so passionate and raw. We did things for the magazine that we would never do for our friends or even for ourselves. It was our blood, really, that was on those pages.

"The world seemed like such a bizarre place to us, that's why everything we did was wrapped in satire and irony. But that was the spirit of the time." His eyes got brighter as he discussed the best times of his youth.

By 1987 everything was changing, and the Eye went out of business. Like Club 57, it was a moment in history.

He finished his dinner Box, and I finished my sushi.

"Thank you for having dinner with me, Leonard."

And "arigato" to you too, Buddha.

Chapter Fourteen

Laboratory 57

There are too many things to absorb and celebrate. I miss what was before and I enjoy what is now, and I already want to grab what is coming up next. I can't lose the habit of watching "Tom & Jerry" cartoons, and I love reruns of "Hogan's Heroes" and "The Honeymooners." I also watch "Saved by the Bells." I guess I am trying to keep a good sense of humor.

It seems like nothing on TV now is any better than the old shows. That's a subject for psychologists. But many "kids" from the club, even though they were all over 20 years old, had the same outlook. Of course Hollywood had influenced our lives and mentalities. So we showed a lot of films at the club—films that were rarely shown in movie houses or on TV.

First came weekly showings of all the classic rock'n'roll films. Soon after followed the Monster Movie Club. Then the great old cartoons. Ann used many clippings from magazines from the '50s and '60s to illustrate the club calendar, and posters and flyers for the programs. Many movie greats from those decades ended up in Ann's work.

It was all of a piece—the East Village boutiques had started making clothes based on the old movies, or selling used clothing from those eras. On movie nights we dressed in the same kinds of clothing.

A few times we produced "film festivals"—nights where we showed several movies back-to-back, following a certain theme. The best music-related films included "British Beat Bash," "I Could Go On Singing," with Judy Garland, "The Girl Can't Help It," by Frank Tashlin, and "Blank Generation," by Amos Poe and Ivan Kral and featuring Blondie, the Ramones, Richard Hell and the Voidoids, Patti Smith, the Talking Heads, Television and other great New York bands. Our "British Invasion" festival included the films "Liverpool Cavern' 62," Ed Sullivan' 64 with The Beatles," and "The Dave Clark Five."

One special evening was dedicated to Doris Day, our girls' "idol," featuring "The Glass-Bottom Boat" and other of her films, and ending with a tribute to the actress, organized by David Richardson and including the film "Lover Come Back."

The "Teenage Sex And Violence" festival was a hit of 1979, with "Gun Crazy," "Teenage Doll," "High School Confidential," "Wild Angels," "Johnny Holiday," and similar classics. A 1980 festival, entitled "The Other Sexes," included "Therese And Isabelle," "The Longing Woman" by Irving Rapper, and "Un Chant d'Amour" by John Genet.

The Cartoon Festival in June of 1979 (interrupted by a party, "Father's Day For Stanley") gave the kids, set at liberty in New York, a chance to revisit their childhoods with Daffy Duck, Betty Boop, Popeye and all the Disney characters. But other times we showed classic films like Fellini's "Marcello."

We also staged our own "TV programs"—that is, we staged live shows in which we parodied programs we had seen on TV. Kenny Scharf did a convincing interpretation of Lawrence Welk in our version of the famous bandleader's show. More challenging yet was our "700 Club" parody, entitled "The 5700 Club." Joining Pat Robertson for this special edition were those sweet religious hypocrites Jimmy Swaggart and Jimmy Bakker. We decorated the club with pictures of saints, flowers and candles. We played sacred organ music, punctuated with hard rock. Ann was High Priestess, and was surrounded by adoring girls. Ann got competition from Andy and his followers, who argued with Ann over which of America's over 200 religious groups practiced the true faith. He then performed miracles to prove that his sect was the one. He levitated himself to the height of two millimeters from the floor. Ann protested that she couldn't see any space between his shoes and the floor, but Andy remedied that by jumping two feet in the air without any assistance whatsoever.

Andy then squinted his eyes in the crying manner of the famous Swaggart, who used the technique to convince American ladies to send him 70 million dollars. But Andy didn't get any money. In fact, everybody started to scream at him, while they applauded Ann, who was swinging a censer filled with burning incense. But the coup de grace came when Ann showed Andy a certain part of her body, which vanquished him immediately.

Ann then gave a sermon, in which she revealed that she had had a vision: an angel that hovered above the club and told her that from that point on, women can have more than one husband, and that her destiny was to build a great temple in the mountains in California.

"Amen, Amen," everybody yelled.

We also showed real TV shows. One Sunday in March of 1980 we gave a show called "Channel 57," in which we showed videotapes of "Lost In Space," "The Monkees," "My Favorite Martian" and other old favorites. The poster read: "Come over to our house and watch vintage '60s TV shows, with commercials, popcorn and Swanson TV Dinners."

We also had special nights given over to photography. One was called "Shooting Session," in which everyone brought his own camera and took pictures, under the direction of the organizers, Christine Logan, Sherry Rosso and John Moore. In a more serious vein, we produced real photography shows, such as the exhibit of the work of George Haas, Larry Meltzer, Eugene Merinov, Ebert Roberts, Trix Rosen and Harvey Wang.

Of course there were evenings with our main photographer from Hong Kong, Tseng Kwong Chi.

The subjects we saw most were of New York life, Club 57 life and the faces and acts of society. They reflected the present situations and the poetry of our lives. The atmosphere was always friendly, helped by the fact that most of the participants knew each other, and/or lived close by. There were always awards given, though they usually consisted of a six-pack of beer.

We had a lot of special evenings. After the fire at St. Mark's Church on the Bouwerie we sponsored many of their literary events. We had literary events of our own as well. One was a "coalition of amateur poets," or the "Poetes de l'Invisible," featuring Robin Crutchfield, Terri Hardin, Leslie LaRue, R. McCoy, Mark Nasdor, March Penko, Jonathan Shipman, Joe Voitko and Christian Joiris.

On February of 1981, over 40 artists came to participate in "The 57

Performance Expo." All kinds of performance artists came, but poetry and a photography show were the star attractions.

Meanwhile there were plenty of stupid and crazy evenings we cooked up just for fun and to kill time. One night had a talk show format, in which the featured guest was a guy named John Savas who claimed that rock music had cured his cancer. Another evening was called the "Night Of Idiocy or The Model World of Glue," presented by Henry Jones. This night consisted of Henry giving everyone glue and paper and encouragement to build model airplanes, or perhaps just paper sculptures, using their imaginations. One guy who decided to burn his model got a little water dumped on his head.

Soon after that we had a similar effort, an evening of plasticene art. As the designer Dan Friedman said in the book "Art After Midnight," "They had an incredible amount of playfulness. Even if you weren't formally involved in putting the shows together, you could instantly slip into a role. They were expanding their boundaries, altering and pushing them around by creating fantasy environments. They were also the dearest, sweetest most decent people I'd ever met. It was almost like they were good Americans in a classic sense."

That's just what it was like, too. Just imagine the "Night at the Opry"—a happy evening of country music, led by William Fleet Lively's band. The whole crew dressed like the Broadway play, "Annie Get Your Gun." Or the nights Pulsallama played. Pulsallama was a 13-member girls' percussion band, which took up most of the girls in Club 57. Most of the time they were all yelling, screaming and beating pots to rhythms taken from Indian songs and others they made up themselves. Or "The Dating Game," which ended in a huge pillow fight.

Another night I like very much was the "Art Evening," in which all the members of Club 57 performed in some manner. Ann sang what she wrote, Andy sang a number from the movie "Ben," and Jeffrey Geiger sang a show tune. After I heard him sing I became angry at him. "Why don't you produce your own shows?" I scolded. Why don't you go to music school? Why don't you …" But Jeffrey was a shy boy in spite of his great talent, with no connections in the music business, and so he just said, "Stanley, I'm not so great. You are the only person who can put me on Broadway, but you have no opportunity to do so. So I will wait until you can."

Everything was permissible that didn't hurt someone else. But the only nights I can think of that did not have the sting of irony and parody were Chanukah and Christmas. To me they were like a vacation from the pranks of misbehaving children. Maybe this was because everyone was missing the warmth and togetherness of their childhood days.

Christmastime we sang carols and dressed in the "normal" middle class style. One person would start telling a story about his town, another about her home. The first time I celebrated Chanukah it was with Jeffrey Geiger and Naomi Regelson. These were actually two quiet angels about whom I did not write too much. But they always came to the club and participated in its life. If anybody really gave me a feeling of honest friendship, it was them. I got enough hugging and kissing from them and enough warm words. Thanks, Naomi and Jeffrey. You were the smile of the club and the smile of my life.

The yarmulke, made of a shiny fabric, kept falling from my head. Naomi told me I could take it off, but I said, "No, I won't feel like I was fully participating." So she got a bobby pin and attached the yarmulke to my hair.

That evening I heard a few words of Jewish wisdom (some of which reminded me of the Communists in Poland): "What will become of the sheep if the wolf is the judge?" And: "A wise man knows what he says; a fool says what he knows." Or: "The tongue is the pen of the heart."

And Naomi soon became the pen of the heart as the DJ of a radio station.

Thanksgiving was celebrated with a show in which John Sex was the only turkey that wanted to be eaten. A few girls tried to do it, too.

But this turkey wore a Mexican sombrero which I had given him upon my return from Tijuana.

Scott Wittman and Marc Shaiman, the writer and composer, were a special pair at Club 57. They created many musical shows and theme evenings, putting their youthful vigor and enthusiasm at the service of East Village society.

Their acerbic humor, very much welcome at the club, first showed itself in their parody musical, "The Sound Of Muzak." Almost the entire Club membership was involved in this elaborate performance. Naturally, no financial profit was gained from our tiny club. But when you are young, you believe in friendship and fun. And that was what everyone had plenty of at Club 57.

In June of 1980 they produced "Club 57 Goes to the Catskills," a revue containing music, storytelling and lots of Jewish humor. The best story came from Marc:

"There was a very poor tailor who couldn't afford to feed his six children. Unable to find any peace of mind, he went to the rabbi for advice.

'Rabbi,' he said, 'I can't stand my miserable life any longer.'

'It's a good thing that you came to me,' said the rabbi, 'I want to help you, not only as your religious leader, but also as a good customer of yours. You always make such good clothing for me. If you listen to me you will be happy again.'

'I will be thankful to you, especially if it quiets my poor, complaining wife, who is like a wasp flying around my ears.'

'It's going to take a while, and it's not that easy. Tonight, bring all your chickens to live inside the house with you.'

The tailor did as he was told, even though his house was one of the smallest in the village. 'I did what you told me,' he reported to the rabbi, 'Even though it's very messy in the house now.'

'Be patient!' urged the rabbi. 'Tonight bring the goat to your apartment.' The tailor did thus.

'And how is it now?' asked the holy man of the tailor.

'Rabbi, it's so horrible now that it's impossible to live.'

'Patience! Now bring your cow inside.'

'Inside the house with us?'

'Absolutely!' was the sage's advice. 'And so it must stay for the rest of the week.' The tailor again did as he was told.

Two days later, the rabbi heard the tailor praying in the sanctuary most piteously: 'Oh God, help me! My life is a Hell on Earth. Please take me, for my life is over!'

The holy man called the tailor over to him and said, 'I told you to be patient. Now tonight take the chickens out of the house.'

'And how is it now?' he asked the good man the next day.

'Better, Rebbe, but it's still very noisy and dirty, and I can't do my work.'

'Take the goat out tonight.' The tailor rushed home to do as he was instructed.

Two days later the rabbi again inquired.

'Better, Rebbe, but still pretty bad.'

'Tonight take the cow out of your house.'

The next day the good man rushed over to the rabbi's house. The holy man went out to meet him. 'And how is life?' he asked.

'Oh, Rebbe,' exclaimed the tailor. 'Life is beautiful.'"

This inspirational story will always stay with me.

Another memorable production was of a play called "Boing Boing," written by Scott and organized by Scott together with Andy Rees and Marc Shaiman. The action of the play took place in Bernard's pad in a better section of Newark with eight actors: P. Dougherty, Ula Hedwig, Tracy Brod, Scott Covert, Georgia Wise, Lisa Passaro, Tracey Berg and Bill Gallo. Scott and Marc grew up with both talent and success, they went to Hollywood in search of a dream and returned to New York with a Tony award for their work on the Broadway show Hairspray.

The living characters of Club 57 were also immortalized in the drawings of Daniel Ethan Abraham, a dapper young cartoonist whose detailed line drawings captured the members in humorous but loving caricature. Daniel and other artists who worked with pen and ink more than with paint were a big part of the Club 57 esthetic, perhaps even more than the painters were.

Speaking of the Club 57 esthetic, it did not remain just at the club, but, like the smell of good cooking, it brought club owners and producers from all over New York. Steve Mass of the famed Mudd Club, Rudolf Piepper of Danceteria, and Steve Rubell of Studio 54 all came running to feed on the energy of the young Club 57 members. Before long they had recruited key members to perform, program events and create décor for their own clubs. Ann Magnuson, John Sex and the others began reaching larger audiences (and receiving real paychecks) at these and other venues across the nation, and overseas as well. By the mid-1980s, nightclubs, galleries, universities and arts centers were all competing against each other to sponsor the Club 57 artists and others like them who had created a new way of viewing art—and the society it reflected.

When Andy Rees became the new manager, he continued to absorb new artists into the club, mixing their work with that of those who came before. He introduced himself as manager in a very Club 57 way, by producing an evening presenting his life, illustrated by his family pictures.

His next official act was to begin printing a newsletter, The Club 57 News. What he did over the next several months we can see printed in the paper.

"VIDEO SCOTCH-GUARD promises a compilation of presentation in this ever-growing medium. Featured is <u>Barry Shills'</u> documentary of the agony peculiar to delinquent youth. A product that has consumed three years of Mr. Shills' attentions. Also … tapes by <u>Keith Haring, Bruce Birbaum, Kenny Scharf,</u> and <u>Target Video</u> … Keith Haring's open color Xerox, yet another hallmark study in contemporary enterprise, premieres on September 15th. {featuring} Etch-A-Sketch, Spin Art, and Colorforms …

" …Whatever is wrong with U.S. theater, there is certainly no lack of handsome new community playhouses and energetic young performers. An evening of stimulating encounters hosted by <u>Scott Covert.</u> Monologues, duets, poems, songs, improvisations. Scenes from Albee, Shaw, Wilde, and Mummenschantz. Has <u>Vicky Schrott</u> ever been afraid of Virginia Woolf? …

"Watch on the 19th as Hugh Hefner's dreams of flesh stalk the Playboy Bunny Lounge. All tits, all ass, all <u>Ann Magnuson.</u>

"Also—the Sex, Sin and Sadism film Festival …

"September 13th—<u>Bikini Girl Magazine</u> Party, featuring OOH-LA-LA ONDINE …

"<u>Stanley,</u> our own Stanley, invites all on the Club 57 Field Trip …"

Here's what the New York Post had to say about some Club 57 shows:

"If you can't spring for the Broadway musical "Nine," how about seeing "Trilogy Of Terror," starring Laura Kenyon, one of "Nine"s most delectable divas. This is an uproarious musical satire of 'women living on the edge,' and it's done in Roto-rama (you rotate your seat after each scene) … The bad news is that it's usually sold out so you many have to stand. The good news is that standing room only costs $4.99 …"

So many events—I didn't tell you half of them. Like a never-ending circus, maybe a Roman circus sometimes. Anyway, it was the best part of my life, thanks to you Club 57 kids. Sometimes I think of how many artists went through that tiny, ugly, small room looking for a chance in New York. Hundreds. And what we made happen there.

Chapter Fifteen

The Beautiful Girl

On the southwest corner of St. Mark's and First are two semi-permanent fixtures. One is a shoe store. The other is a girl. She is beautiful. She gazes at the city that is her home. The long lines of expensive cars authenticate the richness of this nation. Like the lines of applicants at the U.S. Immigrations Department downtown.

The sun shines off the shimmering leaves of the acacias, with their white flowers that together with the leaves, rejoice in the warmth of the sun. The old houses jealously look at the beauty of nature. But, cuddled by the warm sun, the old houses don't look so ugly, even though all of them have the same flat roofs and iron fire escapes. The sun rises from the East River and Tompkins Square and it is not until noon that it hits the colorful mural on the wall of the shoe store where the girl is standing.

And on the sidewalks walk attractive boys who pass her with a smile. How many of them dream to hold you in their arms, beautiful girl? How many of them envy the sun that kisses your lips and your white arms?

I passed this girl often on the way to my apartment, like many boys and girls I know have done. There under a mirror stands the TV, companion of the lonely apartment dweller. The picture is bleary. The glass of Tropicana orange juice cools my nerves, my brain and, finally, my heart. I am watching the TV news. I must see the weather forecast. But for the weather report, I would not be watching TV at all. I don't know why TV has become so ugly to me. Maybe the producers think it's good. I'm sure the stations want good programming to increase their commercial viability. Therefore is seems like some kind of a weird secret why they play on the public's lowest instincts.

Since there's no National Geographic or Nature show on Channel 13 today, I turn the TV off. I have sufficient strength to avoid watching much TV, and not become a dirty rag after television's washing. But what about the children?

The phone rings. It's Terry, my kid. I don't know how I chose him from so many others to be a part of my personal life. Certainly his unusual enthusiasm fascinates me, his ever-smiling face brings me happiness, brightens my days, gives me respite from the tension of dealing with the two clubs, 57 and Irving Plaza, as well as the restaurant and my sister Danuta, who always comes to me with her problems. But it's not only that. What talent he has, what an ear for music! Any song he hears, he can immediately play on his Farfisa electric organ.

The Farfisa is my favorite instrument. His band, "The Living," contains his twelve friends. It's very important for him to have them all together with him like Jesus' Twelve Disciples. He wouldn't want a smaller band. I don't know how he can have two girlfriends in the same band, but he does. What kind of relationship do they have? Some kind of symbiosis like the sun and its planets, with a lot of interpersonal tolerance. He doesn't live with his true love. He lives with Nancy, whom he calls Schmantzy. Like a little kid, he gives his own names to his friends. Another he calls Plum.

Terry has long hair and looks 16, though he is 20. Schmantzy is like a mother to him, but he also calls her "Sister." And that's how they feel about each other ... or is there more to it?

Terry has called because he has something important to tell me. Everything he has to tell me is "very important."

I had wanted to see the news. It is depressing to me. TV pushes itself into man's brain, creating an ultra-reality that fills his eyes with garbage.

Several policemen have been arrested in Brooklyn for collaborating with drug dealers. Who knows how many of them are still at large, an integral part of the drug trade. They're well-organized and leave few traces. It's just too lucrative to quit. It has put down deep roots. What gardener will be able to dig them out? And we might as well ask, What gardener allowed these weeds to grow? Where is the limit to this demoralization of society?

Is it your fault, teenagers of the nation, that you don't yet know how to find the good? You are fed tolerance of crime and pornography; gangsters, drug dealers and murderers are portrayed as idols. And this is supposed to be "for their good." Liberals are all too willing to let them know "the truth," which is supposed to make them happy. But how can you give it to little kids who have barely learned to speak?

Terry is like Salai, Leonardo Da Vinci's kid. Just ten times worse. And I am not Leonardo. He says he is going to visit his mother on Long Island, and needs $20. Or he has a toothache and is short $30 to see a dentist. Or it's his birthday and he needs a new pair of jeans.

He used to work in my restaurant on First Avenue. Now he works for Leshko's on Avenue A. He should be making enough money for his expenses. The only money I spend on him is for his band's rehearsal. I've agreed to be his manager. I even asked Ann to cancel a concert at Club 57 to make room for his band's debut. This was 1980.

The band's debut was a success. Terry wrote all the songs and music, and they were well-arranged and well-played. He knows that his success is mine too, and his joy is my joy.

After the gig I go to the dressing room in the basement, I grab him by the ears and plant a kiss on his forehead. He is sweating. A friend who used to work with him now gives him something that doesn't look like chewing gum. Terry looks at me, abashed. He takes the little plastic bag filled with white powder and empties it into his hand, then sniffs the contents into his nose. Cocaine. Now that he has gotten everything he wanted, my heart and my help, he stops covering up. "This is only for fun, Stanley. Everybody uses it sometimes to relax."

I looked at him without saying anything. I just left.

Yes, now kids like to play with powder, not with a baseball. Everybody does it. For fun. Sure, the President of the United States should do it too. Just wait, you'll see it.

Right now the Beautiful Girl is at the corner of St. Mark's and First. She also hangs out at other corners, St. Mark's and Second, Seventh Street and Second Avenue, 14th and Second. Her eyes are wide open and shining, sad and serious. What is she doing, why is she always on the street? I'm coming back from shopping and she looks me full in the face. "Do you have any spare change?" Why is she always short of money? And why isn't she ashamed of asking for it? A beautiful girl like her can get a job easily.

She must be hungry. So I open the shopping bag and say, "Take what you want." She gives me a strange look and suddenly, turns around with great animosity and walks off. What did I do wrong? And why is she begging if she's not hungry?

A meal she can get anywhere. But she needs money for a needle and powder. The smallest dose of heroin costs $10. She has to take the medicine of her life, and she will beg until she reaches the hearts of the passersby, until she can get that for which she is hungry.

A beautiful girl who became part of the landscape of these streets. A sad landscape. How many girls like this have you seen in America?

And what is Terry doing? He has started to smoke grass in my presence. Officially, as it were. And he tells me, "Stanley, you should smoke it too. You can't sleep. After some of this you'll sleep very well." It's true that I sleep very little, and when the dawn comes I feel so apathetic. I have a great thirst for sleep, but it doesn't come. I've started to feel the need for sleep more than for food, drink or sex. And it won't come.

Hot milk doesn't help me, nor do pills, a hot bath, natural herbs and all else science has to offer. And now I'm worrying about Terry too. So I try some pot. Once, twice, three times. Marijuana is not as strong as I thought it would be. Pall Mall cigarettes are almost as strong. Terry gave me a roach clip, which are sold all over downtown, especially in tobacco and candy stores. We shared it. Like everybody does. Maybe Terry wants me to be his partner in his high times.

But pot doesn't help me at all to sleep. On the contrary, I feel like I just drank a strong cup of coffee. It clears my mind. Soon I don't want to see any more grass. I think there are better things to spend money on.

It is now early 1980. Terry visits me often. Sometimes he locks himself in the toilet for what seems a long time. After he leaves I see burnt matches on the floor, and burn holes in the carpet, more each time. He takes a black bag with him as if it holds some treasure too valuable to leave behind. Once by mistake he left his Pandora's box behind, and I took a look inside. There were matches, a length of soft rubber tube, a little candle, a blackened silver spoon. And the cobra:

a needle. I choked on my saliva. Terry is taking heroin. It was my tragedy too. It made me think of the book by Theodore Dreiser called "American Tragedy." But there is no comparison. Drugs are the biggest tragedy America has ever seen.

It all blew up in a big "victory" for Terry and his heroin. Terry stopped coming to see me for a while. Then he started showing up again. He'd look in my desk, or even in my pocket after I'd tell him I didn't have any money for him. One day his "sister" Schmantzy came to see me. She had a kind of flush on her face.

She knows Terry is using drugs, she says, but she doesn't know what to do. He even forced her to do drugs with him. His mother has come up from Florida. She wants to take him back with her to get him out of the New York scene for a while. But she's short about $200. Can I lend it to her? I not only can—I must. Anything to take him out of that place where he is ruled by drugs. His mother even wishes to see me, Schmantzy relates. Terry has told me that his mother has wanted to meet me after having heard so much about me. But now they're in a great hurry. I gave her the money.

Now here's a surprise—everything was just a big lie. His mother never came to New York. They had no plans to go to Florida. Terry and Schmantzy just wanted money for a great heroin binge.

I called a few days later to speak to Schmantzy. Terry picked up the phone and hung up immediately upon hearing my voice. After a minute Schmantzy called back. "Stanley, it was me. I was expecting someone else to call and for a joke I changed my voice to sound like Terry's."

"You can tell it to another idiot," I shot back, "Not me." And I hung up. Terry ran over to my house a short time later. I finally realized that our relationship had run its course. I then knew why Terry lived with Schmantzy like brother and sister. They had some kind of convent going where God was a drug.

"Stanley, I love you," Terry whined. "I don't want to break up with you. I won't use drugs anymore." But his eyes were looking everywhere for money whenever I left the room for a minute. Any money he could get his hands on. Even two dollars, five dollars would be enough to buy valium. Anything to satisfy that hunger.

After we have a meeting about it, they agree to sign up at the local methadone clinic. So they're now getting substitute heroin. Not much of a cure. First we go to a hospital in the Bronx, then Schmantzy finds one close by at Astor Place. I went there many times to check if they were really on the program. Sometimes they were, other times not. These times I forbade him to see me.

About this time I decided I must make my life easier. I closed both my restaurant and Club 57 at Irving Plaza in July of 1980, and began to travel, to see the world.

So here I am in Egypt, then in Israel. Holy places. And I'm praying, for Terry. More than anyone else. And here I am on Golgotha, praying for his mother whom I never met, at the spot where the Mother of God held Him in Her arms after he was taken down from the cross. I closed my eyes and imagined Michelangelo's Pietà. Then I took a leaf from that place as a memento. To remember the pain suffered by the Mother of God. In memory of the pain which crucified Terry and his mother and myself. And this pain never left us.

So the Beautiful Girl walks the streets and begs. Who is so hardhearted not to give change to such a pleasant girl? Maybe she can't work. Maybe she's sick. Or maybe she needs medicine. Yes, she really needs it for medicine. Don't give her change, because she needs money only for her strange sickness, for injections.

And now there's someone else on steps of some house on St. Mark's Place. His name is Andrew. I know him longer than I know anyone else on this street. He likes and has a certain respect for me.

"What's new, Stanley, how are you?" he asks.

"Fine, thank you. And what is new in your life?"

"I just got out of jail. I got caught stealing. Mostly I do it with a lookout, but he escaped and they got me. We do it all the time. We get radios and electronic equipment, clothing, or even meat from the supermarket. Anything is good to us. We sell it for a few dollars, 10% or 20% of what it's worth, just to get money as soon as possible and get high. Sometimes they catch us and put us in jail for several months. We do a lot of crazy things in there to get high too. Now I'm really broke." So I bought a pizza and we ate it together.

"Andrew," I asked him, "tell me what is so special about heroin."

"I'll tell you. When you shoot up … you can't imagine such a wonderful, marvelous feeling. Nothing in this world is better. You don't care about anything—your mother, your brother, your friends or you lover. Nothing can spoil your mood. The only thing that can spoil it is lack of heroin. You don't worry about food, a place to sleep or live, art, nature, or your country. You don't worry about how many people you hurt and how many suffer. You have no respect for anybody, only maybe your friend who is sharing drugs with you."

"And how about sex?"

"I probably forget about it. I'm not interested in it."

"And nature?"

"I don't care what's going on around me. I don't see the beauty of the world. My world is beautiful." He smiled. He must have been on drugs, because he wasn't nervous.

I wanted to know more. "How about love, and the people who love you?"

"I don't care about anybody. I told you already. I know that people love us. So we use it as one more way to get money from them. We know all the tricks, and we know the weakness of people who love us. We can give them a lot of misery."

"How do you get the stuff?" I asked.

"There are many places. You can buy it on 11th Street behind the brown door. You can't go too far inside. The door is open. In front of it there are kids who give a signal to someone on an upper floor. Then you go inside the vestibule, where you can only see a hand take the money. Then you have to wait until it comes back with the stuff.

"The best place to buy it is on Rivington Street. I'm going there tomorrow morning. If you wish you can come with me. Then you can see the whole operation."

The next day I went with Andrew to Rivington Street. 7:30 a.m. Everything is organized. Boys are out on the street calling "Black Sunday, Black Sunday." Every few days they come up with a new brand name. Some Wall Street types would arrive first. They have to get there before work. Then comes anybody who wants it badly. The selling is quick, giving little time for observation. They know that at 8:15 the police will come … with plenty of notice. It's hard to say how many police are involved in this shadowy world of corruption. But all of them know what's going on, including the higher-ups, who "absolutely don't know anything." There's even a special word, "rat," for a policeman who's against it.

What hope is there for those on heroin, and those who love them? Probably either to suffer without hope, or to rupture the connection forever.

Andrew bought his stuff. Then we got breakfast and he went to use the toilet in my apartment. I'm sure it was to shoot up. But not only that. He wanted to prove to me that everything he said was true. The next day I came home from work to find my apartment had been robbed.

Around that time Terry was preparing for a new gig with his band The Living at the Underground nightclub. He was very busy with the rehearsals, as well as running around to cop drugs. At times I thought he had quit. But once he blurted out to me, "Stanley, even if I've finished using heroin, I'll always try it again. At least sometimes, on a holiday or for my birthday. It's something I can't abandon completely, and nobody can help me or understand me in this." Yes, addiction to that hallucinogen was greater than his music that he loves, more than friendship of his friends, more than love of his mother, more than pictures that he liked to paint, more than any joy of life and life itself.

For the show at the Underground the band wore very modern and really new wave white clothing. Only he looked different. He had on a white shirt and white short slacks in a style from 50 years ago. He cut his hair Marine-style for the first time in his life. I was angry because of that, because he lost his boyish looks when his hair went into the basket. But the whole show surprised me. It was really very good. Everything was made by him—the clothing, the songs and the performance. Add to this the spirit of friendship from the people who love him and work for him. The impression on me was great. And not only on me. A promoter from South Africa was affected, too. He wanted him to work in a series of shows there. But I wasn't involved in that. Terry didn't talk to me for several weeks. He was mad because I "didn't help him" for the show by not giving him $50 for drugs and thereby almost ruining his show. Of course, having his "talent," he got the money from somewhere.

So I had some peace for a few weeks, but I missed him and worried about him. Then one day Schmantzy knocked on the door. I opened it. Behind her was a very "shy" boy. Schmantzy said, "Here is your kid. Better take him. He missed you very much." The kid came to the room and quietly said, "I want to be with you. I need a quiet place that nobody will bother me. Only with you I can feel safe and comfortable. I have to prepare for my tour of South Africa. I got the contract. The promoter wants a good portfolio of my band. I want to do it in your apartment. May I?"

So he stayed in my apartment. The naïve promoter started paying him a beginning salary of $500 a week. At that time it was a good salary. Terry did the portfolio in a few weeks. It looked like it was too long and not so effective. My apartment was very messy, full of magazines, pictures, papers and glues and pencils and all kinds of tools with which you can make very big projects. His friends even came to help him. In the end, even without having much experience, he did it. He created a pretty good portfolio. All the time he was talking about canceling his tour to South Africa, in protest against the official racism that existed at the time.

One day when I came in, Terry was lying in bed groaning. As usual there was no place to walk between the artwork, papers and clothing. He started to whine and toss on the bed. I held his body and massaged his legs, which were thrashing around a lot. Then I gave him some milk. He just groaned, "Stanley, please help me." Then he suddenly tossed his hands and head, and struck his hand on an Indian wooden screen that stood next to my bed, and his head hit the sharp corner of the bed. Again I massaged the muscles of his legs and hands. Then I put plasters on his cut forehead and hands. He calmed down. "Stanley," he said, "You are so good to me. Thank you,"

That night Terry didn't sleep. He was making a cardboard box. In the morning he gave me it and said, "This is for you, Stanley. Keep it to remember me by."

The box was in the form of a cross. You don't often see boxes in the shapes of the things inside. I opened the box. Inside was an old burned cross he found somewhere in an old East Village building. This cross is always with me, together with Terry's life and his pain. And my wife hasn't thrown it out yet. Now she knows I like the things from the time when I was young, the secret story of my life, which was so varied: from happy to tragic times. It was my life, the way it was. I can't change it. I learned my wisdom from it and I am trying to impart a little to you.

Terry went back to Schmantzy. She visited me soon. I asked her what was going on.

"Stanley," she said, "The money he got from the South African producer ruined him completely. I don't know what to do now."

"I don't know either," I replied. "Look for a good doctor or clinic." She left.

Terry came the next day and begged me to lend him $20. I refused. Of course that $20 he needed for heroin. That's how he spent the $2000 a month with Schmantzy. They had the best time. They had so much money and they knew what to do with it. And now Terry was asking and begging for more. "No!" I yelled. He yelled too:

"That's how you love me? You let me suffer?" My brother was visiting me and was very much confused. Terry didn't see anything, only that 20 bucks that I refused to give him. He took the lamp from the night table and threw it on the floor. He started to kick everything around him. Then he looked at me and suddenly ran from my apartment, slamming the door as if insane. "This is my kid," I said to my brother, "I will take care of this. He's sick." My brother saw how he was sick and we didn't talk about it anymore.

Evening time Schmantzy came to me for advice. "Stanley, only you can help him. I'm going to the clinic and I'm OK. Anyway I'm going to Germany for a long time to be far from New York. It should help me. Tomorrow I have an appointment with a doctor at Mt. Sinai Hospital. Take him with me please. A good friend made the appointment for him. They have a new medicine better than methadone." Next day Terry came with Schmantzy and we went to First Avenue to get a taxi.

On the corner there was the girl. She looked at Terry and he said, "How are you?" to her. You see they knew each other. The same class. Then he screamed to Schmantzy, "I don't want to go with him. I don't." He couldn't stand me, he hated me because I said no to him when he wanted $20 for drugs. It was too much for him to understand my feeling for him without giving him that kind of support.

But I refused to pay the fee for the doctor if I couldn't go. At last he agreed and we rode to the hospital to 102nd Street, Mt. Sinai Hospital. He was supposed to be there for two weeks under tight control, then visit a clinic for addicted patients near to the hospital, and take the medicine every second day. I went to the hospital twice to bring him fruit. They wouldn't allow him any visitors. After five days he escaped from the hospital, taking his clothing, by using his tricks. Somebody was even bringing valium and pot to the hospital for him, he told me later. He had so many good friends and he knew how to manipulate them. He knew how to lie, and he explained that it would help cure him.

But I brought him back to the hospital, and the doctor sent him immediately to the clinic to get medicine. Three times a week. I told him I would be there too three times a week. I was going to check if he was taking the medicine and watch how he swallowed the pills. I didn't believe even the nurse who was giving him the pills, he could put them down his shirt instead of into his throat. Several weeks passed like that. Schmantzy went to Germany to lose her habit and to work. Of course the promoter from Africa stopped paying him money the day he suffered the attack in my apartment.

Once I took Terry rowing in Central Park. We boated around the lake near the angel fountain, then under the Bow Bridge, then to the rocks. I was rowing. He looked around like it was his first time in New York. Fall was just beginning. The trees were colorful and leaves were starting to fall slowly to the ground. But it was a sunny day and light white clouds moved in the sky, sometimes like a veil covering sharp sun rays. In the park it was pretty quiet. It was before noon. This time of day and year there are much fewer people. We felt our bond to nature freely. The billiard ducks were swimming around, and ballcocks did circles around them. The leaves on the lake were like spots from an impressionist painter's brush. The trees of course were very different in size and shape, and all of them were losing their leaves. Sometimes some fish would jump over the mirror of water, giving evidence of a secret, hidden underwater life. There was life everywhere. Birds on the trees, flies, bugs, and above all the squirrels. They really have much to do in preparing their food for winter.

The Springtime is so different than Autumn, but Autumn is also as busy in the park as in the forest. And colorful if not due to the flowers, but from a wide spectrum of yellow and orange leaves. And the birds also make much noise, if not because of love. Harvest time is also joyful for them as for people.

Terry is looking around with his wide-open eyes; some bug is trying to sit on his head, then on his nose. He smiles. We don't talk too much. I know he likes to be here. At least now I see him naturally happy. When was he here the last time?

"Stanley," he said, "It is wonderful here. I haven't been to the park for a long time. I forgot how gorgeous the world is. I didn't realize that nature exists and you can be happy with it. Can you visit my Grandma's house on Long Island? It is beautiful there too."

So next Sunday we went to Long Island, by the Sound. The house was wood, built only for vacation time. Nobody was living there. We walked around and he talked about his family, his childhood, and the many times he spent here with his family and friends.

"The water, Stanley," he explained, "When it's high tide, we can swim easily in the bay. Then, during the reflux, we ride the current to the mouth of the bay. The bay is always flowing, like a river. I was feeling like a free bird here, running around the sand hills and the bushes. I wish you could spend time with me here. I could write my music and we could draw pictures and read books. And eveningtime we could walk on the shore to wash our feet in wet sand and smell the wind coming from the ocean."

It really would be superb, but I have to be in my New York. The days when we spent time in Central Park and Long Island were the best time I had with Terry. He's now trying to live in Long Island with his mom. His dream to be famous is gone—temporarily and maybe forever. His band doesn't rehearse anymore. His habit brought him nowhere. He can't think realistically. He's very nervous. I only saw him occasionally after that. He had many misadventures without me. I'm not sure if he ever finished with heroin. I met him once buying smoke at the corner of St.Mark's and First Avenue. He said had to have at least some pot instead of heroin. Maybe so.

Once I brought him to 54th Street to show him the swimming facilities there. He promised to go at least twice a week. I don't know how he is now. I will always miss him and love him, like everybody whom I've loved in my life, but I can't be with him anymore.

There are two more corners on the intersection on St. Mark's Place.

The third one is the location of the St. Mark's Bar & Grill, and in front of it a man was killed several years ago. The other corner is where Stromboli Pizza is, where the Club 57 kids ate their daily meal, tasty, healthy and not so expensive. Most of the time when I am going home I cross First Avenue from the "pizza corner" to the "smoke corner." It has been so many years that the same fat girl has been selling smoke. She must have good stuff, because she has a good business. When I came out of the hospital few years ago I had difficulty walking. Everybody would have to go around her because she stood in the center of the sidewalk with her bodyguards. I asked her to stand a little to the side so that I could walk straight with my cane. but she replied, "I use the sidewalk as I want. I pay taxes too."

"Yes, I know to whom you pay taxes," I answered. She is the queen of the sidewalk, with her soldiers all around.

In 1981 it was still fun at Club 57. Ann and I never tolerated drugs at the club. We concentrated on art programs and this gave us much satisfaction. If there was any drug activity we'd know it. But of course we suspected some our members used them. Maybe marijuana or sometime cocaine. I think most everybody had some experience with it on a small scale.

Heroin was a different story. People who use heroin are very strange and can be identified very easily. Heavy drug use didn't go with the atmosphere of the club. Our people wanted to get somewhere. Most of them were students or college graduates. They had high aspirations, they were too intelligent to get heavily into drugs and give themselves over to hallucination. There was more of a tendency for drugs to get those who still were going to college, or never finished. I learned later that if drugs were used it wasn't at the club but in private life. Well, most of the time anyway ...

In 1981, when Ann quit as manager of the little Club 57 to concentrate on her performance career, I hired Andy Rees to take her place. Thing went well for a few months. Then ...

Next year, 1982. Me:

"Andy, how come we are losing money? How come you are so dizzy? Why are you so rude and aggressive toward all your friends?"

Club 57 choir: "He is using drugs, Stanley! Are you blind? Drugs, drugs, drugs, DRUGS!!!"

Andy: Stanley—I love you. Don't hurt me. I want to work for you!"

My heart was crying, but I said: "Don't kiss my hand, please. Just give me the keys to the club."

I couldn't stand this and I went swimming to cool off. Soon I hired Ira Abramowitz.

Next year, 1983. Me:

"Ira, how come we are losing money? How come you are so dizzy? Why are you running around naked at night at the club? What is that needle doing behind the bar?"

Ira: "Stanley, I was tired and I stayed overnight at the club. It was so hot … I didn't see any needle. Don't hurt me. I want to work for you and the club!"

Club 57 choir: "He is using drugs, Stanley! Can't you see? Drugs, drugs, drugs,

DRUGS!!!"

My heart was crying, but I said: "Don't hug me, please. Just give me the keys to the club."

I couldn't stand this and I went swimming to cool off.

Then I started thinking: What had I accomplished during these five years at the club? Did I achieve anything at all? I didn't make the church any money. I didn't make any money myself. I didn't make anyone else rich. Five years of fighting with life. What did I accomplish, besides providing a shooting gallery for Ira?

And so, drugs contributed to my decision to close Club 57 in February of 1983, as we will see.

Only the Beautiful Girl still walks on St. Mark's Place. She never went to the club and she doesn't know what it was. But she is going to that brown door where probably the last of the Club 57 kids went. You see, they have something in common. But she is not neat like she was. And the passing handsome boys don't smile at her. There are more and more of them, and more lovely girls passing like a stream through the East Village; it has become a new, young, energetic, never-sleeping place. Which of those girls will end up like that one? She doesn't have the strength to move her hand for change or to look at anybody.

Only her shadow tells us that at one time she was a human being.

Wednesday, September 19th, 1994, Channel 7: Barbara Walters, the famous newswoman, is running her program, "Turning Point," in which she talks about police corruption. Just a few days ago a large group of policemen involved in the drug trade were arrested. I recall the Bible, how Heaven was created and the angels of Heaven revolted against the Lord's rules and started to serve darkness and evil. They became angels of darkness. Then I recalled the police corruption of several years ago. The police chief created new regulations, switching the officers' location every few years to control corruption. The police demonstrated in the streets. They started job actions, neglecting to hand out summonses. The City lost a lot of cash, and the Police Chief was forced to retreat. The officers won't disturb their "second jobs." Maybe that's why they are against the Guardian Angels and made war against those nice boys.

Barbara is talking about Frank Serpico, the policeman who refused to serve the Devil and fought against corruption during the '60s. Then she spoke about Michael Dowd, who in 1993 released a report about the strange behavior of many policemen involved with drugs.

The police hierarchy first ignored him and then persecuted him because he wanted to be honest instead of a dirty rag. Barbara is now talking about the Mollen Commission, which had great success in discovering a gang of criminal policemen in action.

These cowards are going to church every Sunday with their children and explaining to them how to be honest men. They teach their children morality, they want them very much to be happy, but are they going to be happy, seeing their parents washed out with immorality and shame? They don't worry about the children of their fellows, children of friends and neighbors.

"Over many years," Barbara Walters says, "Nothing has changed." We discover only a small percentage of police crime. But not every policeman is bad, she says. A great hope?!

September 29, 1994. The New York Times: "Until now only 30 officers from the 30th Precinct have been arrested. Today 14 more have joined them. And for that first time, supervisors face changes." And what about the church to which they go every Sunday? According to me, not much except lamentation. But churches and temples must be doing something more besides decoration and words. This is not the Middle Ages. People, especially the young, are educated and want to see love, to touch love, to feel love. It is not true that God is somewhere in space. He lives in the heart. If you don't have him in your heart you would be suited to work in the New York Police Department, where corruption reigns.

Barbara was very careful. She said most of the police officers were good men. If so, I wish them all the best, except maybe those ones who beat the homeless and sick people in Tompkins Square Park. Yes, religious people don't care too much that Jesus was walking on the water two thousand years ago. They're looking for Him on New York City streets, like He walks with Mother Teresa in Calcutta, like He was with Dr. Albert Schweitzer in Africa. He wants to come to the Bronx too, I'm sure, and first, what He wants to do is to visit the 30th Precinct in the Bronx. I know it, He told me that.

On one of the four corners of St. Mark's Place stands what's left of the Beautiful Girl. She has gotten her sickness, anorexia nervosa, because she didn't have money to buy food. All the money she grabbed from naïve pedestrians she used to feed the children of the Mafia. She is giving them all she has to buy drugs. Hanging from her body are dirty shreds of pants. On her feet she has no socks, just ragged tennis shoes. On her bony arm hangs some blouse. What is that on her head? Is it hair or a dead animal? Nobody will touch it now. How many boys wanted to kiss her lips? Many. Only these are not lips anymore, but some hole with rotten teeth and foul saliva. Do you remember her lovely eyes, that were looking at the wonderful world of her youth? Now there are only foggy glasses that don't see anything. She doesn't have a heart anymore to love anybody. Her eyes don't see flowers, they won't see birds, or the sky. They don't see that new wave picture on the wall of the shoe store where she is standing every day. The eyes won't see you when you pass by, even when you are giving her a quarter. Her eyes don't need those things and they don't see the beauty, joy and dreams, as if her dried soul was jabbed by the needle of heroin. She is dead, even as she walks. If anybody suffers looking at her it is probably your heart when you pass her, and maybe some good spirit who is waiting to take her from that vale of tears and despair. And her mother, if she knows where she is, is the only one who will kiss her and give her a hug of cuddling.

But what about the other types of crime? I don't have anything against the National Rifle Association. I would like to belong to them and enjoy the pleasure of being in forests and be part of the wild feeling of hunters, like Hemingway. Sometimes that wild feeling of adventure comes to my heart too. Nature is strange. I don't trust myself sometimes. I want to be so kind to every creature that I don't want to kill even a fly, then I wish to hunt for great animals. It's a conflict of conscience.

Anyway the Association members have many rifles in their hands, and nobody wants to stop them. The Bradley Bill was intended to control criminals' access to weapons. But the NRA protested. Hey, we have to start somehow to regulate this destruction, and I think that the Bradley Bill would be a small step. Have some common sense! Don't rush to give a gun to the hand of everybody with a tendency to murder and crime. Limits! If that's too much for you free Americans, then at least agree to limit the crime. The gun is now too much in fashion among youngsters. On the same raw front page of the Times you see that Nicholas Heyward, 13 years old, was killed by policemen. It's not the kid's fault not the policeman's. Only our society that makes toy weapons popular. The policeman I'm sure suffers more than you think.

He is in shock. Nicholas was so young, handsome and talented. But not anymore. Mayor Giuliani attended the funeral. I voted for you, Giuliani, to be Mayor of New York, and helped you in your campaign. Can you be stop being afraid of all the different Mafias? Can you be yourself and show how you are a great man, not a small dwarf Narcissus spreading your arms in a gesture of helplessness? I voted for you because you are New York's hope. And one more thing. Can you make it that instead of the President's picture hanging in New York's police precincts there will be one of the Beautiful Girl?

Billions of dollars of ours are flowing for crime on TV, demoralizing not only teenagers but little children as well. The TV criminalists say, "Watch what your kid watches. This is a free country. We didn't tell your children what to watch. It's a matter of free choice."

And I don't know that cunning and perversity was greater under communism where I have been and know it, or on American TV. If not for the weather broadcasts, I probably wouldn't watch TV at all. The news doesn't have any balance between good and bad. There is only crime, which is squeezing into the brains of innocent children. You even make fun of it here, like Joey Adams does in the New York Post.

Can you imagine New York several years from now? All windows barred or bricked up. Iron doors with many locks and alarm systems. Crime and anarchy throughout New York. The rich people who created this chaos don't live here anymore. Only their managers coming here to process the business and contracts with the crime world, or pay the bribery. Police drive in armed cars and little tanks. But police stations are behind citadel walls. The mayor of the city is a well-known mobster, chosen by threatening the poor people.

The main festivities are wonderful parades of all the Mafia families, street gangs and drug traffickers. Also present are delegations from a few South American countries with their official armies. Everybody in the White House is corrupt and uses free supplies of drugs of every kind. New York is divided into zones of influence. Large maps of New York in their offices show the fighting between their gangs, who no longer hide themselves. Children and youngsters are very proud to belong to them. They watch their great heroes like Al Capone, whose statue stands in the front of City Hall as a great American hero who fought against the odds. All this is in the name of free expression of everybody's personality and needs. There are TV programs of gang fights on the streets. You can see it on the TV, where during commercials they tell you which drug is the best for any kind of feeling. And they set the price of drugs on the world market. Nobody can protest now officially against the true freedom of American life given by Washington and Jefferson two hundred years ago. Free spirit maybe terrorizes some part of society, but there is nothing bad that can't turn out to be good, especially for society whom without any reason at one time was called immoral. Now we have new morality and the world is ours. We gave freedom to the world, except the Muslim religion, which doesn't allow the use of drugs. So we all live only once. Isn't it true? I tell you we have our own philosophy, too. You remember Stanley? He said too, it's better to live shorter and good than longer and without fun, something like that.

On the weekend the Mafia bosses move to their "dachas" outside of New York. There they're going to the churches with their families. After the service they're throwing a party for all parish members, giving a great donation for the churches using the money they have from crime. They hope that when they die the church will put a memorial plate in the church for their generosity, and after the weekend they come back to New York when they feel better, with some heads of temples who secretly bring Beautiful Girls to parish nightclubs where they can enjoy the new lifestyle for rich and famous.

Everybody pays a special tax for "security," almost like in Moscow in 1994. Whoever wants to come to see the museums or Lincoln Center has to pay a "security tax." Everywhere you can see modern technology. There are no private taxis or cars on the main streets, just comfortable free electronic wagons with small stores inside selling soda, sandwiches and drugs. Everybody has a videophone and can see the person to whom he is talking. The streets are very clean. You see, the new City Council is high class. People who don't or can't use drugs are tolerated and nobody harasses them. The only thing that they have to do is to clean the streets in the morning, because the Sanitation Department doesn't have to do it, being busy playing cards and sharing money and drugs. A few years ago the policy of their existence changed and they now use their stations as drug depots.

In the supermarkets they have many new kinds of food, and liquid meals created by the Japanese, concentrated food. Just drink a glass and it will keep you strong for fighting and terrorizing people if you're a mobster, or to work hard if you're just not smart enough to belong to the new "True American Freedom Party." And for fun you can play with the bones of the dead. It's a new game, attractive, costing little but having many fans in the city. The new City Council is holding a Spring conference. The big issue for the Department of Education is what to do with stubborn teachers who harass kids who use drugs and guns against them. They know that free expression gave American kids the highest marks in science. The teachers have been told to leave the kids alone. They know everything now, you don't know anything. Don't bother them; they can be sick and unhappy. Also on the conference agenda is the problem with St. Patrick's Cathedral. The Cardinal doesn't want to sell the Cathedral for a nightclub. That club would be very attractive and can bring in the top clients, drug events and big money. Even though the church pays security tax to the city. The Council is very much for having the club there. The mass can be in the morning and the club will be only from 10 p.m. And the city is ready to cut the church's tax rate.

There is also problem with the United Nations. The City Council wants to permit every country's drug lords to operate free around the world. Everybody understand that natural human right except for a few Muslim countries and China. Where did they find their morality? Certainly not in the free world. And there might be a war. Some country's lords of drugs have nuclear weapons. And the Chinese too. The New York City Council is so popular throughout the world due to its efforts in trying to solve the problem and cool the hot parties. They solve so many problems, including approval of bribery and corruption. Nobody who makes money will go to jail. It wasn't right. Many years ago there was a mayor of New York City named Giuliani. He tried to fight the system but was afraid, he didn't have a noble character and enough strength. He gave up. Some kind of American hero. His name is not commemorated on the city streets. But next month the city will pay tribute to a few great names of criminal kids who already killed some teachers for fun and in the name of the "New Wave Cultural Revolution."

Or maybe that noble-faced General Colin Powell has become president? I badly want it. And maybe it will be like in the Bible but the opposite way. And the fallen angels from Chicago who prefer to serve the drug dealers will start to serve their community and country. Who I knows? Unknown are the roads of history.

O! America! The world looks to you. You are the model and its hope. The world needs you to help to fight evil. But do we hire a thief to watch our house? You are not as bad as I wrote. But wake up. I want only to watch good news on channel 13. You are the hope of your girls and boys. They are looking into your eyes and hope you don't hurt them. If I love you, America, it's because of them. You are the hope of the world whom you have to give a good example. But this chapter won't have a happy ending, because you were the hope of the Beautiful Girl, too.

Chapter Sixteen

Contemporary Pietà

"The only way to be protect yourself from this disease is to use condoms ..." The voice of surgeon general Koop is very serious and determined. He throws heavy words of truth into the mind of society. The news rapidly got to the root of the matter. But more rapidly, AIDS was harvesting its crop.

People diligently watched the news. People cried over the new plague on humanity. Phonies, cynics and hypocrites condemned the victims.

At the club everybody is talking about it. But these people didn't go to the baths or the dark rooms at the "just sex" clubs. That's what I was thinking. Or did they?

One day I went on the M15 bus toward East 66th Street, and there I saw Klaus Nomi, who lived on that block. It had been a long time since I had seen him; the last time was when his manager wanted two thousand bucks for his performance. They wanted to go very fast to the country of financial success.

We couldn't talk, because of the crowd. He looked at me and nodded. He did not return my smile. His face was pale and the spots on his face terrified me, the same spots I had just seen on TV. Oh, God, I was stunned. Then suddenly everybody at the club knew that Nomi had gotten AIDS. Yes. He was going to New York Hospital for treatment. What kind of treatment? A study. The shadow of sorrow swept away the free and easy smiles of the club members.

For a long time it seemed nothing followed the initial shock. The baths did not want to close their "free sex" business. Somewhere in the evolutionary development of the world and humanity, Mother Nature had decided to show her teeth to the sexual revolution.

I saw Klaus several more times on the bus uptown. He never smiled. In his eyes I read tragedy and the question, "What next?" Once it was difficult for us to avoid each other: the bus was empty. We talked, not about AIDS and death, but about life.

"You have the best friends in America anyone could imagine," Klaus said to me. "Tell them that they are my best friends, too. It doesn't matter what happens with me. They participated in the best adventure of my life, in the beginning, during 'New Wave Vaudeville.' I think that in that tiny club, the enthusiasm of youth was highly concentrated. It was also a celebration of beauty in art, and friendship. At that time we were looking for goodness, and a place in American society, in New York. I miss everybody a lot."

"You made a big mark in the East Village, especially at Club 57, with all the 'Vaudeville' artists," I answered. "Do you remember your first great performance at Irving? You wanted a bigger mirror in the dressing room so you could put on your makeup. It took a lot to make it so classy. Your face became your trademark, like Keith Haring's 'Radiant Baby'."

He didn't feel comfortable talking so much, but he wanted to return my respect for him, so he said, "I am from a German family and I wanted to be friends with someone who was Polish. I remember when you stopped us from throwing that cross on the floor of the stage and took out that part of the show. I think at that time you were more mature than we were. You understood that a cross or a star or an American flag meant too much more than just a piece of iron, wood or fabric, to just burn it."

At that moment we both understood how much we needed each other's respect. Especially the respect of two men for one another. One sick, one healthy, one German, one Polish, who in the end were special friends. I didn't see him after that. Anymore. You know what that means? His mother came from Germany, he died in her arms. It was a picture I think of as a "Contemporary Pietà."

A shudder of death passed across the East Village, and across my mind and soul, too. The film, "Torch Song Trilogy," showed the misperceptions and the hysteria of the times. There was endless speculation, helplessness and misunderstanding. There was a guy who had AIDS who wanted to use a public swimming pool, and the people closed the pool. There are kids who are sharing pens in school, putting them in their mouths. There are kids who share the same needles. What about kissing? Can we get the virus from that? It depends on what kind of kissing. Did I kiss someone, or hug or eat from the same plate or drink from the same glass? Yes. We are like one family, we play family games here. The East Village, my family town. Why do I have some brown spots on my face? The doctor said, "Everything is all right, but your diet is very bad. Too much sugar—you are close to getting hyperglycemia. You drink too much ginger ale and cranberry juice." Hysteria, hysteria, hysteria! Not only mine.

"What about my difficulty breathing?"

"Just a blocked artery." Yes, I wanted to work three shifts and make a million dollars, to build a financial empire with the kids. Even with safe sex I got what I asked for. Nobody stopped me from playing a dangerous game with nature, who caught me red-handed. Now I won't have anything—no money and no health.

Only my wife stays with me and won't leave under any circumstance. She wanted to make money, too. But, like me, she pushed too hard, and has found many obstacles. She wanted to buy a house and a better car. But I don't want anything anymore, just peace. It is not coming, instead comes more news. Jean-Michel Basquiat is dead, from an overdose. His best friend wasn't Andy Warhol, it was heroin. He got lost in the "underground crime capitalist system," which, with great success, is devouring America's children. Could the statue of Saint George come down off his pedestal in front of the United Nations headquarters and slay that dragon, I ask you?

The voice of "First Lady" Nancy Reagan is just as naïve the Reagan administration's whole drug-fighting program. But the tentacles of this lady reach very far, including the White House and the television industry. The White House pretends it knows how to use its overflowing riches, for splendors and ceremonies. For Christmas trees and slogans like "Just say no to drugs." Some people mask their hypocrisy and helplessness with symbols. For a few shining moments they can cover the truth. For this, thousands of kids are giving their lives. Why annoy the Mafia? Don't you know what happened to the Kennedys?

I have no peace anymore. Even with the heat of hysteria gone, the problem isn't. We learn we can't get it from touching or talking, but we know that many children are sick. And women too, largely due to the increasingly popular bisexual lifestyle, which will never leave the closet. Freud always said it was more popular than most people believed.

More and more people die of AIDS. More people get sick. More people protest against the gay lifestyle. Keith Haring and ACT UP fight back, invading St. Patrick's Cathedral during mass. I forgive him that. But what do you expect from the Church? Change the dogma, the two thousand year old tradition? Even the Pope can't do that.

The Church opens its arms for those sick with AIDS. The main work of the Church is to give love to the poorest of the poor. But even the Church got sick during the Inquisition. What can you do when even your good friends don't want to see you?

In August of 1989, Rolling Stone magazine was an open platform for Keith. It showed that he was the most open, honest person you could hope to find. In that piece, Keith became a free man. He told the story of his life, exactly how it was, without hypocrisy, bigotry or cynicism. Now we know why everybody loves his paintings so much, why he had so many admirers. It didn't matter what kind of person you were, Republican or Democrat, yellow or white, Christian or nonbeliever. We badly need honesty. He spoke out; showed us how the emperor was naked. He became our hero, with as much bravery as Hercules. There are not many like him and maybe never will be.

Now Keith, the "son of humanity," was dying, surrounded by friends and family, his mother at his bedside like so many other mothers holding their dying sons in their arms. At that time I was in Florida, enjoying the beaches, the sunshine and the sunsets, thinking about who I was and why I was alive after my heart attacks and heart operation, and why Keith died. I think he died for my life and the lives of others. When I came back to New York it wasn't for a good time. I had to go straight to Beth Israel Hospital where my good friend John Sex was waiting for me, just a few blocks from my home.

"I can't go with you," said Susan. "I am afraid of everything, I have children." So I went by myself to the hospital. John looked at me. "Glad to see you, Stan. I got pneumonia."

"You are a troublemaker," I answered, stroking his foot. "I told you many times not to run to the subway with a light jacket in the wintertime. I told you to put on a sweater or the leather jacket that I gave you. You didn't listen."

"You were right. Now there are complications, and I have to stay here longer."

"I just left New York Hospital," I said. "I am no better off than you. I didn't listen to nature, not to overwork. We are both bad kids. I didn't pass the test for Paradise, I'm still alive. The nurses tried to send me there anyway. Especially that nurse who took care of me after my operation. She pulled the tube from my aorta, and blood was pouring like a fountain. She was busy talking to her friend about how bad her coffee was at lunch. I knew something was going wrong. I yelled at her to pay attention, and she finally turned around. Later, she complained about what a difficult time she had with me. Some nurse. At least I was luckier than Andy Warhol."

I was talking to John about my latest problems to make him more comfortable with his. I hoped that would make us come to an understanding. "Thanks for coming," he sid. "I heard that Ann is doing very well in Hollywood."

"She is recognized as an East Village star," I told him. "She came to New York almost the same time as Madonna. Everybody has different luck. I came here as a poor man, too. My first job I got a dollar an hour. You know what? I still have a dollar in my pocket," I started to joke. "I paid too much for my experience."

"You became a 'Star of Life,'" John replied. "I'll tell you something. If not for you, there would never have been a Club 57. You were always crazy."

"Of course it took a lot of work to keep the club alive. It was my own 'Radiant Baby.' We were all that crawling baby. We knew it. That is why Keith's art was so close to our hearts. We were moving against the tide in a world full of hypocrites and snobs. That's why we tried to stick together."

"I apologize to you, Stan," he continued, "in {Steve} Hager's {book} 'Art After Midnight,' I was joking about the broken chairs at the club, that wasn't fair."

"There are many things that are not fair," I said. "Why didn't you go to a new-chair-place like Studio 54?"

"I wouldn't have gotten so many hugs. That Hager book didn't show you much respect."

"Maybe I wasn't so great. You were the kids who gave me so much happiness, that's what counts. Some day in the future, when we meet again, I want to be with you."

"Do you believe in heaven?"

"Yes, sure, it is very easy to see it with your own eyes."

"How do you do it?"

"Just open the door. To do it you have to have a key."

"Where is the key?"

"In your heart and mind. If you can feel goodness and beauty. If you have the good will to help others. It will take time, but you will see heaven."

John was happy with my answer but he changed the subject. "Tell me something about Susan's children, Stan,"

"I just saw them a few days ago," I said. "We went to a Mexican restaurant in Greenwich Village. Margaret is a very talented painter. At Christmas she always makes me a colorful picture. Charles is a storyteller. He will surely be a writer. I've asked him for a story about a couple, with a beautiful flower and the Sun." John was listening with his eyes closed.

"Susan's ambition is to have two famous kids. This is how life is: If we aren't lucky enough to be able to afford to reach our dreams, then we can try to help our children to do it. I wanted to have children."

John had fallen asleep. His breath was calm and even. I didn't have to talk anymore. The nurse gave me a sign that he would be sleeping for awhile. Is this the last time I will see John? I kissed his forehead. Goodbye.

John, one of my best friends, died the next year, at a time when our government and Congress were taking a splendid vacation. It was also the time I was taking mine, playing badminton, watching the surfer boys and bikini girls at Copacabana beach in Rio. The time when I went to the grandest statue of Christ in the world, searching for His help. It was just cold stone built by some Polish architect. Wherever I looked for Him, He wasn't there. He had said it Himself: "Whatever you do to your poorest brother, you also do unto Me." That's where He is most, in the hearts of the poor.

Susan is a center of information for me. Since I closed the club, people would call her, to have a last chance at touching the club's happy days, but these messages aren't so happy. The photographer from Hong Kong, Tseng Kwong Chi, who made pictures of the New York lifestyle, and who one evening played Elvis Presley, has died. I have coffee with Susan somewhere near her apartment on 82nd Street. "Stan, it really drives me crazy. I think there's nobody from the club and this bisexual East Village who isn't sick. Your manager Andy Rees died. The last weeks of his life he got crazy, yelling at everybody, 'I want to live! I want to live!' Oh Lord, why are you taking the kids who haven't fulfilled their lives yet?

Then I said to her, "Sex is the biggest gift nature gives us. It is also to have fun. We can't ignore it, or avoid it. We have to respect it. We have to make it sacred. The problem is how to handle it with wisdom. We can learn from Freud, Kinsey, or even Dr. Ruth, how to handle our own private needs, thirsts and dreams. We are all so different in this matter."

Days later, the phone is ringing. It's Susan. "Someone else, Stanley. Do you remember that girl ..."

Chapter Seventeen

Quotations

NY Rocker, May 1978, by David Koepp

"Yeah, New York is *Fun City.* And the Zantees and the Fleshtones playing the 57 Club on St. Mark's Place is Fun City too. Kids were boppin', jumpin', twistin' and shoutin' to this wonderful rock and roll. It was a strange and beautiful night; you could almost feel your sweat dropping to the beat."

Wow, Fleshstones! You made me crazy. You never played better than you did that night.

***

The Soho Weekly News, May 25 1978, by Roy Trakin

"The tiny 57 Club at 57 St. Mark's Place is located in the basement of the Polish Catholic church between Second and First Avenues. An affable fellow named Stanley runs the place and handles the concessions at the shows, working the bar with a glee that reveals his affection for the kids and punks who jam the cave-like club and pogo into the night."

I looked up 'affable' in the dictionary. Is it possible not to be affable? I don't think so.

***

Melody Maker (London), 1978, by Stanley Mieses

"Suicide headlines a benefit programme at the Club 57, a new venue that has been booking good shows consistently, considered along with Max's and CBGB's as the top new wave clubs in town. [...] Prior to Suicide, who were well-received, bio-feedback violinist/musician Walter Stedding droned on, apparently to the delight of Debbie Harry and Robert Fripp, who joined him onstage for the Saturday evening performance."

It was the middle act, the B-52s, who stole the show. Oh yeah, the B-52s!

***

City Hall

June 19,1978

Dear Mr. Strychacki,

It is my understanding that representatives of your organization have met with Susan Herman, the executive Assistant to the Director of the New York City Youth Board. If you wish your program to be among those considered for funding next year, I recommend that you submit a letter of intent to the Youth Board.

Sincerely,

Edward I. Koch

Mayor

It was me who met Susan, and you too.

I couldn't wait 'til next year. I started the club myself. Thank you. Anyway, you are a great mayor, and I like you very much.

***

The Village Voice, October 23 1978, by Robert Christgau

"Excitement can happen anyhow, as in the unexpected melee at Club 57.

THURSDAY: By 7:50 there is a formidable line outside Club 57 – that's right, Stanley's Club 57, although in just what sense it's Stanley's remains unclear – for Patti Smith and Sam Shepard's *Cowboy Mouth*."

Robert, you forgot to pay for the beer.

***

The New York Times, March 30 1979, by John Rockwell

"If you like to dance to rock music, a good place to be tonight is Club 57 at Irving Plaza, 17 Irving Place at 15th Street, where from 9:30 P.M. on Richard Hell and the Voidoids will hold forth. Mr. Hell and his mates are among the leading (if not the most distinctive) practitioners.

But the real attraction is the scene itself, about the largest-scale gathering of punk/new wave rock to dance to. Admission $5, 475-9671."
***

New York Times, April 27 1979
"When they do so, several times a month, they create what is probably the biggest of all the rock disco, because the Irving Plaza, with its large floor and balcony area, can accommodate a lot of people. Club 57 rents the place when it has a fairly hot band, and between live sets there's recorded music for dancing."
***

AMERICANA, The Datsun Student Travel Guide
"Club 57 is one of the best rock 'n' roll theaters in the world. It occupies an old vaudeville palace, so the stage is enormous, the auditorium vast and high-ceilinged; ornate chandeliers hang above the balcony. [...] Here you'll meet kids from Brooklyn, Queens, Long Island, New Jersey ... Club 57 is *that* large and *that* popular."

How can anyone belittle the club? Everyone knows it's the best in the cosmos.
***

Soho News, June 1979, by Crispin McCormick Cioe
"Mitch Ryder was a full voice last weekend at the wonderful Club 57 on Irving Place. In a bit of '70s nostalgia Friday night, a naked female admirer streaked onstage to embrace Mr. Ryder from behind. You guessed it, folks, he was in the middle of 'Jenny, Take A Ride'."
***

East Village Eye, June 15 1979, by Lisa Baumgardner
"On St. Mark's Place, the Monster Movie Club, headed by Tom Scully, meets weekly at beautiful old Club 57. Field trips, newsletters, and surprise goodies are promised, besides the unbeatable bargain of one or two classic fright flicks for a mere dollar, if you're a member! This is a wonderful way to organize our youth, diverting their energies from the streets to the appreciation of home movies by Mrs. Bela Lugosi, just prior to the old geezer's death."
***

Punk Magazine, 1979 Contest:
"FIVE STARS FOR CLUB 57"

***

Daily News, July 11 1979, by Patricia O'Hare

"Between June 5th and July 5th of this year, Robert Patrick might easily have been the most performed playwright in the city. Probably his most noted work is "Kennedy's Children," [performed] at the Club 57."

***

Soho Weekly News, August 16 1979

"St. Mark's is exile: The last word in the Poetry Project/Club 57 series will be heard tonight."

***

A card:

Dear Stanley, we want to thank you for your nice present. Everyone had a great time at the party (including us) and we were glad we had it at Club 57!

Thank You,

Robin and Steve, the Visitors

***

History of Modern Art, by H.H. Arnason:

"Not until the 1980's however, did the underground world of self-taught graffiti writers, mainly from the Bronx and Brooklyn, come into direct, interactive contact with the above-ground, Manhattan-based realm of so-called "mainstream" artists or art-school students. The interface occurred primarily in the small experimental nightspots of New York's East Village, such as Club 57."

The young artists could relive their not-so-distant childhoods, listening to a jukebox with New Wave rock, staging performances in the manner of old TV variety shows. They can also mount one-night exhibitions of their art, influenced by the current semiotic interest in popular signs and symbols or old Hanna-Barbera animated cartoons. In this "funky-retro" mood, the SVA crowd also began to hatch anti-Minimalist and anti-Conceptualist ideas, ideas that took on real substance when the graffiti writers showed up, attracted not only by New Wave records but also by the opportunity to meet the art students.

Keith Haring and Kenny Scharf have soared to international

stardom, talking with them Jean-Michel Basquiat – a genuine street, not subway artist but one self-taught from the models of Picasso and African art – as the Graffitists with a capital 'G'.

***

Summons #287529 0

The people of the State of New York vs. Stanley Strychacki.

Place of Occurrence: 57 St. Mark's Place

Offense: Unnecessary noise

Complaint's Name: D. Christopher

The person described is summoned to appear at the Criminal Court of the City of New York.

***

Another card:

Dear Stanley, thanks very much for letting Michael and I come to the B-52s. We think you are great! Good luck in all your pursuits!

Michael & Alice of the Visitors

Another card:

Dear Stanley, thank you so much for the flowers. I was thrilled – it's the first time I've ever received flowers for the performance.

Lady Bug

***

A poster on a tree:

STOP CLUB 57. Please come to the Block Association meeting. Wednesday, September 30, 1979 ...

***

"We have a new heaven – Club 57," went the refrain of the song by Kid Creole and the Coconuts. There were some angels who did not rebel against me, and gave me respect for my creation, and to them I say: Thank you!

***

From a letter by Dany, our stage manager:

Dear Stanley,

Before anything else, I should apologize to you for my misconduct at our meeting. My behavior was rude and unruly and not to be excused, I will certainly abide by whatever decisions you hold to regarding my future with Club 57.

My frustration in not understanding the motives that led to my behavior, which I again apologize for. I have a problem with my attitude towards Chris [Gremski].

My thirteen months with Club 57 have been tremendously rewarding. Thank you for everything.

My answer:

Dear Dany,

I always liked you very much. Suspending you hurt me deeply. My decision was made together with my main crew. I don't think it was a good thing to do. I did it for many business reasons. I apologize to you too. Might you forgive me please?

***

Information on a street lamp:

Dear incompatible, insolent, insufferable, insufficient & insalubrious persons of "CLUB 57" alias Church - take your activities to some city garbage dumpsite, or Rikers Island. Such places would welcome the presence of such filth (rats & prisoners)

St. Mark's Residents & Neighbors

***

Note on the wall:

Stanley,

I've always admired you from afar for a long time.

Love, your secret admirer.

I never had time to find out who it was …

***

New York Times, August 17 1979, by John Rockwell

"Club 57 is a little nightspot at 57 St. Mark's Place in East Village. Club 57 at Irving Plaza is a concert series that takes place under Club 57's auspices at the Irving Plaza.

Now Club 57 is expanding its activities by allying with a man named Miles Copeland. Mr. Copeland is an American who lives in London and has involved himself actively in managing and recording British New Wave bands."

It will be a great event in New York. Saturday and Sunday, the Cramps will be on hand. Fashion plus the Model Citizens will perform later Sunday evening and following weeks; The Buzzcocks, The Gang of Four will be at Irving Plaza on Aug. 31 and Sept. 1; Nico with John Cale and Cheap Perfume – Spet. 7, the Reds – Sept. 8, Mr. Cale – Sept. 14-15, Eddie and the Hot Rods – Sept. 21-22; the Police and Wazmo Nariz – Sept. 27-29, Iggy Pop – Nov. 2-3; XTC – Nov. 5-6; Siouxsie and the Banshees – Nov. 9-10; Ultravox – Nov. 12-13; the Cramps again – Nov. 16-17, and Skafish – Nov. 19-20. Pending are dates for 999, Penetration, Chelsea, Monochrome Set, the Only Ones, the Lurkers, and Pere Ubu.

I knew what I was doing. In a few months I'm going to be rich and famous, and we'll go to the top together. There's no business like show business. Wasn't I right, Gregor of the Invaders? Wasn't I right, Mom?

***

At Irving Plaza my manager Alex is fighting with my agent, Copeland. The shows and Club are in a dangerous situation. There won't be any good shows at Irving Plaza like the New York Times said. I called my manager over to the little Club. He speaks vulgarly:

" Stanley, you don't know what you're doing. I am the manager now. Now it will be different – *you* have to listen to *me*."

"You have three weeks vacation from Club 57," I answered, "to cool down."

"Never!" he yelled, and ran out of the club.

But I knew where he ran. I took a taxi and went to Irving Plaza. The door was open, and I heard from the lobby my "best friend" talking nervously in the office.

"Help me. Stanley doesn't know what he's doing. I am the manager of the Club; I do most of the work. I know everything that needs to be done to run a show there. You people don't need him. I will be nice and good to you, I'll pay more rent. I'll tell you a secret: he is a Communist. You can't let him do any shows here. He will blackmail me, he will kill me."

I stepped into the office. But no matter what I said, nothing could help me get my shows on in that hall. It must be that they drank too much vodka together, that they decided to work with Alex. The hall became busy for "renovation," and for my ex-manager Alex's shows.

***

From Alex's assistant Joseph Curtin's letter:

Dear Stan,

A curious closeness between us, at least a sort of deference, brings this second letter. I have in the course of time developed an admiration for your unique affability under which I have finally realized that I shall never know what it is that you are thinking. An inherited love of frankness, then, brings these details if not simply out of consideration for your feelings however enigmatic.

I'd say, now that the club is successful I can split with peace of mind, and, followed by Alex, Stanley says take twenty-five dollars for Joseph, but I give you thirty-five, such kindness I'm sure. You wanted me to raise money for a project, but for whom? I feel very sorry for people, who lie, cheat, watch over people's shoulders and talk about them behind their backs while secreting news and development.

You have your success, Alex has his mess, and I can leave honorably.

I will never be able to forget when, one night few months ago, your friend Judas said, "Joseph, you become so nervous, you didn't use to be." The shock almost felled me. How does one avoid such a state when step by step one hears from and sees do many moves toward a stab in the back?

Best of luck,

P.S.: My fond regards to your mother.

Together with my life project and my life success I lost one of the best men, Joseph.
　　***

A phone call. Don't I know that sweet voice?

"Stanley, we know that somebody whom you trust ruined your success. That man does not deserve to live. If it helps you to get your concerts at Irving Plaza together, just say one word – we'll finish him. We are your best friends."

Heavens! Why do I have to work with so many monsters? They will kill for pennies. "Don't call me anymore, please," I answered and hung up the phone.

The phone rings again.

"Stanley, this is Chris. I have to see you."

He came and said, "I received a strange call. Somebody wants to kill Alex … This is big money. Alex knew what he was doing when he was destroying our future."

"Aren't you Chris the nobleman?" I asked.

"Try to avoid these people if you know them," Chris answered. "I will go to Irving Plaza. I will get you back there."

And the kid did. After a few months, Irving Plaza welcomed us back. We tried hard to do our best. But it was too late. The best bands already went to play at several new clubs that had opened: Danceteria, the Underground, and the Ritz. We never made money. I went back to concentrate again on the little club.

Sometimes it is like that: you trust bad people that appear to be sweet, and you hurt the good ones. Then you suffer yourself. It doesn't bother me that I lost; I did it with my head up. It's just that I feel bad that I couldn't help the sick children in Poland, like I planned. And I couldn't help some of my good friends to print their music albums. And I feel guilty for giving them the feeling they worked for a loser. They couldn't achieve a better life and success with me. Ejh! Nobody? There are a few who became great.

I forgot about a funny story:

One time my best friend Susan, during her interview with Steven Hager for *Art After Midnight,* said: "Tom, Ann and I, as director, created Club 57. It was pretty ugly and creepy before we moved in."

And other untrue stories. Then she called me, crying, and said, "Dearest Stanley, during the interview I got drunk and I don't know what I was talking about. I just wanted to help Ann in her career in Hollywood, saying that she created Club 57. But it is too late to cancel it, because the book is already in print. Can you ever forgive me?"

"Of course," I said. "I am not going to Hollywood. Ann worked very hard and did not need that kind of help. Anyway, she was the best."

MISFORTUNE IS THE BEST TEST OF TRUE FRIENDSHIP.

Chapter Eighteen

Beyond Heaven

I was watching the weather report on TV and thinking about the dreams I had last night. They made me smile. The dreams I mean. At the same time I was writing down an anecdote about John Sex. One night, while the Misfits played one of their usual loud gigs, a few of the neighbors whom the band had woken up came in the front door to protest. John, who already had a few beers in him, jumped up and yelled, "Good people! Why aren't you sleeping? It's already one a.m.!"

That wasn't all I was doing: I was also eating a tasty cantaloupe. But suddenly, instead of cantaloupe I bit a fork and broke a tooth. Good for me. Didn't my mother tell me not to do several things at the same time? But this is how we live at the end of the 20th century.

By the end of 1981, Ann, Keith, Kenny, Jean-Michel, John Sex, Susan and Tom had all gone on to focus their energies in other areas. They all returned many times to the club, but their careers had forced them out into the world and into the larger society. But this was not the end of Club 57.

Ann was tired of managing the club. As we have seen, her experience had opened the door to other clubs, and she was preparing to reach a wider audience. I didn't protest her resignation.

Luckily, Andy Rees was waiting to fill Ann's shoes. He had helped Ann a lot, to renovate, to bring new good friends and to produce events. Therefore I also chose him to tend bar at Irving Plaza, so he could make some additional money. He started very strongly as the new manager. He didn't want to be compared unfavorably with Ann.

Everything was OK—except for the money. After a few months it was clear that there was something wrong with Andy: there was never enough money to even to pay the church's electricity bill. Andy's eyes were too sharp and shiny. The money was going for his good times. After an investigation by my crew I confirmed that he had started to use drugs. I had to tell him goodbye as manager and bartender. It cost him financially and morally. It hurt me and all the club's kids, who liked him very much. He had been one of the best members.

But it was worse than that. It meant that drugs were coming to Club 57. Andy continued coming to the club. It was his place too. He knew he'd hurt us and he knew we loved him. But it wasn't the same anymore.

I was lost in space. Several weeks went by with me running the club with various members helping out. I was getting sick and depressed. But soon it became apparent that a new star was being born: Ira Abramowitz.

Ira was already involved in the club, and had done some art evenings. He was a very talented organizer, a nice Jewish boy, very hard working, energetic and happy. Always joking, especially Jewish jokes. He used a hilarious Yiddish accent with that special throat-clearing "h" sound that made us laugh to death.

Ira amazed me. He had been assisting Andy, but as it became clear that he was serious about taking charge, everyone, new members and old, rallied around him and helped him get the club back on its feet.

A new spirit came to St. Mark's Place. Ira wanted to do a better job than Andy and even Ann. And I swear, he was doing it. In a few months our financial situation improved considerably.

Ira had an advantage, having the experience of the other club members before him. With them and his own genius, he organized a stream of film festivals, painting exhibitions, video shows, singing engagements, poetry readings, dances and comedy nights. We even had another Sam Shepard play produced.

Ira really wanted to show what he could do. He started to cooperate with everybody to bring people into the club. Now there was a new generation coming there. Ann became a goddess of downtown, and her followers spent their evenings wherever she went. But the East Village was fully alive at this time and we didn't begrudge any newcomers who wanted to do any kind of event.

But the club still needed a boost to get it back on track. We needed money—we owed months of rent money to the church, the space desperately needed a renovation, and we had to pay for new presentations.

Ann and Ira started planning something, but I didn't know what. Only a few days before, I finally found out what it was: the Club 57 Benefit Party at Danceteria.

I swear that Ann, the most tortured and hardest working girl in show business, must have stood on the top of the Empire State building and whistled to all the artists in the city, because they all came from wherever they were to help out Club 57 when we needed them the most. This time, the kids paid me back. What a great feeling to see them all in one place with some thankful feeling for that quiet man, Stanley.

And there I was, as I have said before, happy among young people who really gave their hearts, time, work and energy. I don't know how they became so dedicated. I've never seen any place on Earth with so great a fire of love, concentrated in that small basement at 57 St. Mark's Place.

The whole night there was a constant procession of performances onstage. Ann asked me to give a speech. Choking from emotion, I said, "Thanks very much for your support. You are the craziest people in New York. I will never forget the good times I had with you."

It's strange that I, who was always trying to make money, was the most happy man, not at the time when I made the most, but at the time when I was losing the most.

As I was leaving Danceteria, two young guys asked me if I could get them into the club. They were broke, they said. "I can't help you," I replied. "This is a benefit party organized by the artists, and I have nothing to do with the door." This is how they answered me:

"We played at your club for nothing. And now you show your thanks—you chase us from the door."

I felt like someone had slapped my face.

I can't control myself the whole time. Sometimes I take it all too personally. Maybe that's why I broke my tooth on the cantaloupe that day.

But let's get back to the club. The benefit raised exactly $3,000. Our troubles, however, were not over.

After a while, Ira seemed to lose control of himself. He brought all kinds of people to the club. He'd rent it to anyone, just to make money. I wanted a better program. But it was going down. The program became too primitive—too many wild parties. Ira started to complain about money. Looks like he forgot Andy's story. His eyes were too red and his behavior not too elegant. He was too nervous. I thought it was from overwork. Then the other Club 57 members gave me the true information. Ira had got into drugs. With a great pain in my heart, I had to tell Ira to leave.

By that time I had started to suffer from depression. I was too tired to stay every night at the club and keep tabs on it. I was a dead man from exploiting myself endlessly, and my experience with Terry, the drug-addicted musician, was the last nail in my coffin.

I wasn't too busy by then and I could have run the club myself. It would be a new era. I knew it and the kids knew it. But where was the energy? Gone. What I didn't know then was that the congestion in my heart was the cause of my depression. I called a meeting with Ann and the other founding members. They couldn't or wouldn't step in. The two girls running the bar wanted to take over, but I didn't know them well enough to trust them with the operation.

February First, 1983, was the last evening of Club 57. Bishop John was upset. "Stanley, why have you closed the club? I can't give it to anybody else. You love those kids very much. And they had respect for me. Did I give you a hard time during those years?"

"Of course not," I answered. "You were very understanding, and too tolerant. I think I gave you a hard time, and it is better for the church and the neighbors not to not run a club here. With this new drug environment, it entails too much responsibility. Unknown are the roads of the Lord ... and mine too."

Chapter Nineteen

You Are Only Young Once?

I have discovered many slogans, mottoes and words to live by in my journey through life. For example, for me life is enthusiasm. And I also discovered that the poorer you are, the richer is your life. Of course, that is if you have the inner wish to be a great person. As I recall here the lives of the people of Club 57 and the young people of the East Village, I feel that energy coming to my heart and body. Maybe that is how I have been able, after a few years of struggle, to finish my book.

But I wanted to talk about something else—about young people's suicide. On the cover of People magazine in February 18th, 1985 I see two teenagers from good and not such poor families who poisoned themselves in a Cadillac. Lonnie and Rick. They are so beautiful, so graceful. Then what went on in their brains? The title of the article read: "Why are Your Children Dying? Prompted by a Powerful and Troubling TV Movie."

And this problem is not getting smaller. According to the New York Post in a 1995 article, "About 5,000 young people commit suicide each year, and thousands more have wanted to do it." Another headline screams, "Teen Lovers Drown Themselves In 'Romeo And Juliet' Tragedy." Here are their farewell letters:

"Mom and Dad:
You will never be able to understand the love between me and Christian. Why is it that you will never be able to understand me?

--Marilyn

"To Everyone:
I'm taking my life because without Marilyn I have no life.

--Christian

The pure hearts of young people have difficulties dealing with the problems of life, big and small. And we are born to make this world better. I've repeated it many times in this book, trying to go ahead with my life, fighting and losing constantly.

I also have my love. I was singing my own song of love too:

You are the Beautiful Flower
In the garden of my heart
You are the Sweet Angel
In the Heaven of my Dreams
You are the Song of my Soul
and the Smile of my Life.
Happy the people
With whom you are
I was waiting for you
My whole life
And I always will
Because your eyes made you
My Joy and my Dream.

The Love—one gone from my life. I was devastated, and I thought my life was over. And I started again.

I learn from good people and the Good Books, how to do it. I have many scars on my heart. I learned from the punks how to keep the bus door open when people are leaving. And I also learned from the book of Jewish wisdom: "Money can buy many things, but not brains."

I know what the number one monster is that is destroying young people. It's worse than drugs. It is television. In the name of freedom, these monsters put any kind of garbage into the program. Too many times in my life I have seen devils reading the Bible. Who is brave enough to fight with that powerful evil TV industry? All of us must do so. One president and a few lonely fighters, like Gary Cooper's sheriff in "High Noon," aren't enough.

One of the fighters is Brian Peterson of the New York Post, who wrote in February of 1997, in an article entitled "Marijuana: Trojan Horse": "The beginning of wisdom is knowing what is forbidden. Giving children access to a substance that will damage them is one thing wise people shouldn't do."

There are other magazines on my desk. Newsweek, December 13th, 1993. On the front page: "Global Mafia: They are Ruthless, Stateless, High Tech and Deadly.

" ...In Palermo, Sicily there is a message from the children of the city to the late Mafia-fighting prosecutor Giovanni Falcone: "You have to be a Great Man." Falcone wasn't afraid to fight and was killed.

Now every country has the same problem. Who will run the world in the future? Will it be the way I described it in my New York nightmare fantasy?

Time Magazine, September 1st, 1997:

"Good Cop, Bad Cop: Headlines about brutality have overshadowed the real news: more cities are reining in police misbehavior."

New York Magazine, September 1st, 1997:

"The new Cocaine Culture: Less scary than heroin, cheaper than pot, cocaine is making a comeback."

The New York Times, August 27th, 1995:

"New Front in the Drug War: Seventh Street.

"Why can't you have an officer there at all times?' demanded Jean-Paul Malicsi.

"Are we going to have to hire our own security?' Ms. Joyce asked. 'Is this why we pay taxes?'"

And, finally, from Joey Adams's "Strictly For Laughs" column in the New York Post: "Crime is growing in our town—when you call the local cops, there's a three-week waiting list."

"One day there's going to be as much crime on the streets as on TV."

"Where are we going to put all the crooks today? All the jails and Congress are full."

Sorry, those citations were prepared by me for Tom's Monster Movie Club to scare the public. But it's actually not so bad. The crime rate has gone down recently, along with unemployment. The media have started to do their job, putting pressure on the police. Now the words "police brutality" are not leaving the pages of any newspaper. Is Mayor Giuliani another American hero, keeping his promise to fight the drug lords? Last year on my block there were more drug pushers than pedestrians. It was the "pot center." Suddenly they are gone. The city is going to put a cop near every school. The Big War has started. Good luck, Mr. Mayor. New York Magazine recently asked, "How far can Rudy go?" Maybe to the Presidency, who knows? General Powell disappointed me by not running for President. Along with other Americans, I too am looking for the right President.

I wish we had woken up sooner, and there wouldn't have been the tragedy of Jean-Michel Basquiat and the other unlucky Club 57 kids.

And how about my "wish":

November 18th, 1997: I went to the 6th Street Block Association Garden to see the large wooden sculpture there. I call it a "smile of pop culture," because that's how we feel when we look at it. If art is meant to give the color and sense to the epoch in which we live, then this is art. We get through this simple, naïve, tall structure, decorated by things from our childhood, that we belonged to the world, which is more than nothingness.

The sculpture gave us a smile, coming from deep inside. This year a sculpture by Keith Haring decorated Park Avenue. And in 1998, the musical "Radiant Baby" will try to prove that art, like the mind, is the soul of freedom and humanity. I am looking for it on New York City streets. So I went to Avenue A between 13th and 14th Streets. There the street muralist Chico has painted two women—one very poor and old, and another very rich and glamorous: Mother Teresa and Princess Diana. Such contrast. And yet both of them show why we were born. The two candles burning at the front of the painting are mine. But that Tuesday something happened to my eyes. I saw an angel at the corner of Avenue B and 7th Street, watching over us. Then an old lady named Ann Leone, who had just left the Senior Citizen's Center walked toward him, her shoelaces untied. The angel kneeled and tied her sneakers. I had a camera with me, and I wanted to take a picture of this. But I couldn't. I didn't want to ruin this most divine scene. I can't be another paparazzo.

The angel's name was Officer Ricardo Campos. Could you see such a scene anywhere else in the world? That one cop, together with the joyful smiles and laughter of the small children in Tompkins Square Park, made the East Village more bright and beautiful than the millions of artificial lights in Las Vegas and Disney World combined.

The other problem that bothered the club was sex. Oh, how difficult it is. The problem is giving more headaches to American bishops than to the common people, who take it naturally as it comes.

In the New York Times on January 27th, 1995, Gustave Niebuhr wrote: "Over the last two years, leaders of several Protestant denominations, as well as the National Conference of Catholic Bishops, have taken steps to insure that complaints of sexual misconduct against clergy are investigated quickly and thoroughly."

And this year the Conference Of Bishops issued a statement encouraging understanding and love of homosexuals because they are children of God too. Where did they learn this? Probably from Elizabeth Taylor and Ann Magnuson.

Now I have to confess that I am a very religious man. I have prayed in all different churches and temples in the world, including the most famous places, not because I am a man without a faith, but rather because people all pray to the same God, just in different ways. Do I believe in God? Yes, but I think of Her as a Good Spirit, as when She said, "I am Who am. This is My name." And I saw Her on the throne of Truth, which stands on four legs: Science, Nature, Common Sense and Love.

That is why when Pope John Paul II called strongly this year for respect and tolerance for all different people, I knew he was my kind of man. Bravo, John! From your words and eyes we can see and feel Wisdom and Heaven. I hope the masses will learn from you, not from the Dark Ages. Seems like there's another one I have to register as a Club 57 member. The list is open.

Politically, it could hardly be better. The few local wars around the globe have calmed down. The Mir space station became Club 57 for astronauts from many countries, and the word "Mir" means "Peace." Ted Turner just pledged $1 billion to the United Nations to help kids all over the world. I have a small import business with my wife called USA Super Trade Company, and we're trying to sell the Statue Of

Liberty to the Chinese, and it seems that with the help of that kid Clinton we'll do it.

My mom celebrated her 90th birthday this year with friends, family and of course me, from the top of the Eiffel Tower. And my broken tooth has finally been fixed.

When I put my ears close to the Earth I can hear that Channel Thirteen is making a news show that features only good news, so I can watch it. And producers are fighting over who will get to do the movie from this book. Stop! Don't fight! Wait till I die, then it will be more profitable.

My friend called me a sentimental maniac and said my book wasn't modern enough because I don't use enough words like !@#$%&*. So I must apologize for my un-new wave politeness. This is my parents' fault. Instead of cursing, my father, Joseph, taught me how to draw pictures, and for my birthday my mom was buying me poetry books. Then my friend said, "You're writing many things that have nothing to do with Club 57."

I answered, "How about me? I was the heart and soul of Club 57. Whatever happened to the body, the spirit stays forever. And the spirit is feeling that ecstasy of life that American youth gave me, and extended my own youth. I was young at least twice. Who says you are only young once?

It is already midnight on Wednesday and I have almost finished writing. Why do I feel that I am the words, music, color and feeling of the picture of that time? Is it too much conceited fantasy? Whom can I ask? Maybe the bells of St. Stan can answer me. But at this time of the night they are asleep. I have to wait until tomorrow. I just feel like the "Radiant Baby." Maybe you too?

Good night.

35740691R10113

Made in the USA
Middletown, DE
14 October 2016